Solar Operations Management
Strategies for Success

Josh Rogers

TRUCKROLL

Energy that moves

Disclaimer:

All information is for informational and instructional purposes, asset owners and operators must
adhere to local, state, and national regulatory requirements. Financial guidance is for informational
purpose and benchmarking may be required based on the site specifications and regional market as
trends and factors may impact the applicability.

Table of Contents

This book is dedicated to those leading the transition for a brighter, cleaner, and more sustainable energy industry for future generation

[Chapter 1] - Introduction

The Growing Importance of Solar Energy

In a world facing unprecedented challenges posed by climate change and dwindling fossil fuel resources, the pursuit of sustainable and clean energy solutions has become a paramount endeavor. At the forefront of this global shift towards a more environmentally responsible energy landscape is solar energy—a powerful, abundant, and inexhaustible source of power from the sun. We embark on a journey to explore the remarkable rise of solar energy, its significance in shaping our future, and the pivotal role of those tasked with managing large-scale solar assets.

The story of solar energy is a tale of innovation, adaptation, and relentless determination to harness the boundless energy of our nearest star, the sun. Over centuries, humankind has marveled at the sun's brilliance, but it was only in the latter half of the 20th century that solar photovoltaic (PV) technology emerged as a viable means of converting sunlight into electricity. Since then, solar power has witnessed an astonishing transformation from a niche curiosity to a global energy giant.

Today, solar modules adorn rooftops, fields, and deserts across the world, silently converting sunlight into clean electricity, powering homes, businesses, and entire cities. The rapid advancement of solar technology has made it one of the fastest-growing sources of renewable energy, fundamentally altering the energy landscape.

As the consequences of climate change become increasingly apparent and alarming, there is an urgent need to transition away from fossil fuels, the primary driver of global warming. Solar energy stands as a beacon of hope in this Endeavor. It produces no greenhouse gas emissions during operation, requires minimal water for maintenance, and boasts a minimal ecological footprint compared to traditional energy sources.

By harnessing the power of the sun, nations reduce their reliance on finite fossil fuel reserves and volatile energy markets, enhancing their resilience in the face of geopolitical and economic uncertainties.

Empowering Solar Operations Managers

As the adoption of solar energy accelerates, so does the complexity of managing large-scale solar assets. Solar operations managers play a pivotal role in ensuring the efficient, safe, and sustainable operation of solar installations, spanning multiple sites and configurations. Their responsibilities encompass team development, performance optimization, budgeting, crisis management, and effective communication with senior leadership.

In the pages that follow, we dig into the multifaceted world of solar operations management. We explore strategies and best practices for building high-performing teams, conducting effective meetings, managing personnel and site performance, budgeting for success, handling equipment failures, and communicating with key stakeholders. We'll cover topics that provide actionable insights and strategies for success in managing solar teams and assets across multiple sites.

The Role of a Solar Operations Manager

In the dynamic and rapidly evolving field of solar energy, the role of a Solar Operations Manager (SOM) is pivotal in ensuring the effective and efficient operation of large-scale solar assets. A successful SOM possesses a blend of technical expertise, leadership skills, and a commitment to sustainability.

Defining the Solar Operations Manager

Their role encompasses a diverse range of duties, making them instrumental in maintaining and optimizing solar assets. Here's an overview of their core responsibilities:

Team Leadership:

> SOMs are responsible for assembling, developing, and leading a team of skilled professionals. This includes solar technicians, engineers, and maintenance personnel. Effective leadership is crucial for creating a culture of safety, productivity, and continuous improvement.

Site Oversight:

> Solar assets often span multiple sites and locations. The SOM must coordinate activities across these sites, ensuring that each operates efficiently and effectively. This involves regular site visits, monitoring equipment performance, and implementing maintenance and repair plans.

Performance Optimization:

> Maximizing the energy output of solar installations is a top priority. SOMs work closely with their teams to develop and implement strategies for optimizing performance. This includes routine maintenance, cleaning solar modules, and addressing any technical issues promptly.

Safety and Compliance:

> Safety is paramount in the solar industry. SOMs are responsible for ensuring that all safety protocols and regulatory requirements are met. They must conduct safety audits, provide training, and continuously assess and improve safety measures.

Budget Management:

> Solar operations require careful budgeting and financial planning. SOMs are responsible for preparing and managing budgets for each site. This involves cost control, resource allocation, and financial forecasting.

Data Analysis:

> Solar energy systems generate vast amounts of data. SOMs use data analysis tools to monitor system performance, detect anomalies, and make data-driven decisions for improvements. This data-driven approach is critical for long-term success.

Crisis Management:

> When equipment failures or unexpected issues arise, SOMs must act swiftly to mitigate the impact. They develop contingency plans, work closely with maintenance teams, and ensure that downtime is minimized.

Communication:

> Effective communication is essential for the success of solar operations. SOMs regularly interact with team members, senior leadership, and external stakeholders. They must convey performance metrics, provide updates on projects, and articulate the value of solar energy to various audiences.

Environmental Sustainability:

> As advocates for clean energy, SOMs play a role in ensuring that solar installations adhere to sustainable and eco-friendly practices. They may implement initiatives to minimize the environmental impact of solar operations.

Qualities of a Successful Solar Operations Manager

To excel in this role, a Solar Operations Manager should possess a diverse skill set and certain key qualities:

Technical Expertise:

> A deep understanding of solar technology and systems is fundamental. SOMs must stay current with the latest advancements in solar technology.

Leadership Skills:

> Effective leadership is vital for team motivation and performance. SOMs should inspire their teams to excel and foster a culture of continuous improvement.

Problem-Solving Abilities:

> Solar operations are not without challenges. SOMs must be adept at identifying and resolving issues swiftly and efficiently.

Communication Skills:

> Clear and concise communication is essential when dealing with team members, superiors, and stakeholders. SOMs must convey complex technical information in an understandable manner.

Adaptability:

> The solar industry evolves rapidly. SOMs should be adaptable and open to embracing new technologies and best practices.

[Chapter 2] - Team Development

Building a High-Performing Solar Operations Team

The success of any large-scale solar energy project hinges on the capabilities and cohesion of the team responsible for its operation. Let's dig into the intricacies of assembling and nurturing a high-performing solar operations team, emphasizing the qualities, strategies, and leadership principles that are essential for success.

Selecting the Right Team Members

Building a high-performing team begins with selecting the right individuals. Consider the following when assembling your solar operations team:

Hunger to Continuously Learn:

> Passionate individuals that have a hunger to continuously learn are crucial to the rapidly growing and evolving technology in the clean energy industry.

Technical Competence:

> Ensure team members have the necessary technical skills and qualifications for their roles, including knowledge of solar technology, electrical systems, and maintenance procedures.

Diversity:

> Aim for a diverse team with a range of skills, backgrounds, and perspectives. Diverse teams often excel in problem-solving and innovation.

Cultural Fit:

> Assess candidates for their alignment with the team's values and culture. A cohesive team is more likely to work together effectively.

Establishing Clear Roles and Responsibilities

Define the roles and responsibilities of each team member clearly. This clarity ensures that everyone knows their job and can focus on their areas of expertise. Roles commonly found in a solar operations team include:

- Solar Technicians

- Engineers (electrical, mechanical, or civil)

- Maintenance Specialists

- Data Analysts

- Site Administrators

- Parts or Warehouse Associates

- Safety Coordinators

- Lead Technicians or Supervisors

Fostering a Culture of Collaboration

High-performing teams excel in collaboration. Encourage a culture of open communication, mutual respect, and teamwork. Consider these strategies:

Regular Meetings:

Hold team meetings to discuss goals, challenges, and progress. Encourage team members to share ideas and solutions.

Training and Development:

Invest in ongoing training and development programs to keep team members updated on industry trends and best practices.

Recognition and Rewards:

Recognize and reward exceptional performance to motivate team members and foster a sense of pride and achievement.

Leadership and Empowerment

Leadership is pivotal in building a high-performing team. As a Solar Operations Manager, your role is to inspire and empower your team to reach their full potential. Key leadership principles include:

Lead by Example:

Demonstrate the work ethic, professionalism, and attitude you expect from your team.

Clear Communication:

Ensure that goals, expectations, and feedback are communicated clearly and consistently.

Empowerment:

Delegate authority and responsibility to team members, allowing them to take ownership of their work and decisions.

Conflict Resolution:

Address conflicts and disagreements promptly and constructively, fostering a harmonious work environment.

Continuous Improvement

A high-performing team is never stagnant; it continually seeks ways to improve. Encourage innovation and continuous learning within your team:

Feedback Loops:

Establish regular feedback mechanisms to gather input from team members on processes, equipment, and strategies.

Benchmarking:

Compare your team's performance to industry benchmarks and competitors to identify areas for improvement.

Problem-Solving:

Cultivate a problem-solving mindset within your team, encouraging them to proactively identify and address issues.

Building Team Resilience

In solar operations, teams must be prepared to handle unexpected challenges, such as equipment failures or extreme weather events. Foster resilience by:

Scenario Planning:

> Develop contingency plans and conduct scenario-based drills to prepare for various emergencies.

Adaptability:

> Encourage adaptability and a willingness to learn from setbacks, turning challenges into opportunities for growth.

Building a high-performing solar operations team is a multifaceted endeavor that involves selecting the right individuals, defining clear roles, fostering a collaborative culture, and providing strong leadership. Such teams are not only well-equipped to manage large-scale solar assets effectively but also contribute to the industry's growth and sustainability.

Hiring and Training the Right Talent

A critical aspect of building a high-performing solar operations team is the selection and development of the right talent. Let's dig into the essential steps of hiring and training team members who will contribute to the success and sustainability of your large-scale solar assets.

Recruitment Strategies

Define Your Talent Needs

> Before embarking on the recruitment process, it's essential to have a clear understanding of your team's needs. This involves evaluating the skills, experience, and expertise required for various positions within your solar operations team.

Craft Engaging Job Descriptions

Job descriptions play a pivotal role in attracting qualified candidates. Be sure to create comprehensive job listings that clearly outline roles, responsibilities, and qualifications. Highlight the unique aspects of your organization and the solar industry to entice top talent.

Utilize Multiple Recruitment Channels

To reach a wide pool of potential candidates, leverage various recruitment channels:

Job Boards:

Post job openings on popular job boards, industry-specific websites, and social media platforms.

Networking:

Attend industry events and engage with professional networks to identify potential hires.

Employee Referrals:

Encourage your existing team members to refer candidates from their professional networks.

The Interview and Selection Process

Structured Interviews

Develop a structured interview process that includes a set of standardized questions to assess candidates consistently. Consider behavioral interview techniques to understand how candidates have handled situations in the past.

Technical Assessment

For roles requiring technical expertise, consider conducting technical assessments or skills tests to evaluate candidates' proficiency in areas relevant to solar operations.

Cultural Fit

Assess candidates for cultural fit by exploring their values, work ethic, and alignment with your organization's mission and values.

Reference Checks

Conduct thorough reference checks to validate candidates' qualifications, experience, and work history. Contact former employers or colleagues to gain insights into their performance and character.

Training and Development

New Employee Orientation

Upon hiring, provide new team members with a comprehensive orientation program. This should include an introduction to the organization's culture, policies, safety protocols, and the specific role's expectations.

Ongoing Training

Invest in continuous training and development programs to keep your team updated on industry advancements and best practices. This could involve in-house training sessions, external courses, workshops, or conferences.

Cross-Training

Cross-training team members in various aspects of solar operations can enhance their versatility and resilience. Encourage employees to learn new skills and explore different roles within the team.

Safety Training

Safety is paramount in solar operations. Provide regular safety training to ensure that team members are well-prepared to handle potentially hazardous situations and equipment.

Mentorship and Coaching

Establish mentorship programs to pair experienced team members with newcomers. Mentorship can accelerate the learning process and help newcomers integrate seamlessly into the team.

Diversity and Inclusion

Embrace Diversity

Diversity within your team can foster creativity, innovation, and different perspectives. Actively seek candidates from diverse backgrounds and promote an inclusive work environment where all team members feel valued and heard.

Equal Opportunities

Ensure that your hiring and training practices promote equal opportunities regardless of gender, ethnicity, age, or other factors. Create a workplace that champions meritocracy and fairness.

Employee Retention

Recognize and Reward

Acknowledge and reward exceptional performance to motivate team members and foster a sense of belonging.

Career Development

Provide a clear path for career development within your organization. Employees are more likely to stay when they see opportunities for growth and advancement.

Feedback and Communication

Establish regular feedback mechanisms and open lines of communication with your team. Understand their concerns and aspirations and work collaboratively to address them.

Hiring and training the right talent is a pivotal step in building a high-performing solar operations team. Careful recruitment, effective onboarding, ongoing training, and a commitment to diversity and inclusion are essential elements in this process. With the right team members in place, you can move forward confidently in managing large-scale solar assets effectively.

Fostering a Culture of Safety and Sustainability

Safety and sustainability are the cornerstones of responsible solar operations. Let's explore the critical importance of cultivating a culture that prioritizes the well-being of personnel and the long-term environmental impact of large-scale solar assets.

Safety First

The Imperative of Safety

Safety is not merely a regulatory requirement; it is an ethical responsibility. Solar operations involve inherent risks, from electrical hazards to working at heights. A commitment to safety protects your team, the integrity of the installations, and the reputation of your organization.

Establishing Safety Protocols

Develop comprehensive safety protocols specific to solar operations. These protocols should cover a range of scenarios, including routine maintenance, equipment repair, and emergency response. Ensure that every team member is trained in these protocols.

Safety Equipment and Gear

Provide the necessary safety equipment and gear, such as personal protective equipment (PPE), fall protection systems, and fire extinguishers. Regularly inspect and maintain this equipment to ensure its effectiveness.

Safety Training

Continuous safety training is essential. Conduct regular safety drills and simulations to prepare your team for potential emergencies. Encourage open discussions about safety concerns and near-miss incidents to facilitate a culture of learning and improvement.

Sustainability and Environmental Stewardship

Solar energy is a clean and renewable resource, but its sustainability depends on responsible practices. Embrace the principles of environmental stewardship to minimize the ecological impact of your solar assets.

Eco-Friendly Site Design

During the planning and construction phases, prioritize eco-friendly site design. Minimize disruption to local ecosystems, protect biodiversity, and consider the long-term implications of site development.

Sustainable Operations

Incorporate sustainability into daily operations. Implement environmentally responsible practices, such as water conservation, waste reduction, and vegetation management that supports local wildlife.

Regulatory Compliance

Stay informed about environmental regulations and compliance requirements. Ensure that your solar operations adhere to local, national, and international environmental standards.

Environmental Impact Assessment

Periodically assess the environmental impact of your solar installations. This includes monitoring land use, water consumption, and wildlife interactions. Use the data to make informed decisions about mitigation and improvement.

Building a Culture of Safety and Sustainability

Leadership's Role

Leadership sets the tone for the organization's culture. Solar Operations Managers should champion safety and sustainability as non-negotiable values. Lead by example in adhering to safety protocols and sustainable practices.

Employee Engagement

Engage employees at all levels in safety and sustainability initiatives. Encourage them to take ownership of these values by actively participating in safety committees, sustainability projects, and suggesting improvements.

Communication and Training

Effective communication is vital in promoting a culture of safety and sustainability. Regularly communicate the importance of these principles and provide training to ensure that every team member understands their role in upholding them.

Reporting and Accountability

Create a reporting system for safety incidents and environmental concerns. Analyze the data to identify trends and use it to implement corrective actions and drive improvements. Hold individuals and teams accountable for their contributions to safety and sustainability goals.

Recognition and Rewards

Acknowledge and reward individuals and teams for outstanding contributions to safety and sustainability. Recognizing achievements reinforces the importance of these values and motivates continued excellence.

Fostering a culture of safety and sustainability in your solar operations team is essential for the well-being of your personnel, the longevity of your solar assets, and the environmental responsibility of your organization. You can create a team that not only operates efficiently but also contributes positively to the broader goal of a more sustainable and responsible solar industry.

[Chapter 3] - Team Meetings

Effective Communication in Solar Operations

Effective communication is the lifeblood of a successful solar operations team. Let's explore the importance of team meetings and how they facilitate clear and efficient communication within the team.

The Role of Team Meetings

Information Exchange

Team meetings serve as a platform for exchanging crucial information. They are the ideal setting for discussing updates, sharing insights, and addressing challenges that affect solar operations.

Collaboration and Problem-Solving

Team meetings provide a collaborative environment where team members can collectively brainstorm solutions to problems, share best practices, and offer support to one another.

Goal Alignment

Effective team meetings help ensure that everyone is aligned with the overarching goals and objectives of the solar operations team. They serve as a reminder of the team's mission and purpose.

Building Team Cohesion

Regular team meetings foster a sense of belonging and unity among team members. They create opportunities for team members to get to know one another, which can improve cooperation and teamwork.

Structuring Effective Team Meetings

Clear Agendas

Every team meeting should have a clear and well-structured agenda. The agenda should outline the topics to be discussed, the goals for the meeting, and the expected outcomes.

Defined Roles

Assign specific roles for each team member in the meeting. This includes a meeting leader or facilitator responsible for guiding the discussion and a timekeeper to ensure the meeting stays on track.

Time Management

Respect team members' time by starting and ending meetings on schedule. Allocate specific time slots for each agenda item to prevent overruns.

Inclusivity

Encourage active participation from all team members. Ensure that quieter voices are heard, and that team members feel comfortable sharing their thoughts and ideas.

Minutes and Action Items

Appoint someone to take meeting minutes and record action items. Distribute the minutes and action items promptly after the meeting to ensure that everyone is aware of their responsibilities.

Effective Communication Strategies

Clarity and Conciseness

In solar operations, complex technical information is often conveyed. Ensure that communication is clear, concise, and free from jargon that may be unfamiliar to some team members.

Active Listening

Effective communication is a two-way street. Encourage team members to actively listen to one another, ask clarifying questions, and seek to understand different perspectives.

Transparency

Openness and transparency build trust within the team. Share relevant information and updates, even if they are challenging or concerning.

Technology and Tools

Leverage technology and communication tools to facilitate remote meetings, share documents, and collaborate in real time. Ensure that all team members are proficient in using these tools.

Conflict Resolution

Inevitably, conflicts may arise. Teach team members conflict resolution techniques to address disagreements constructively and maintain a positive working environment.

Meeting Frequency and Types

Regularity

Determine the appropriate frequency for team meetings. While some teams benefit from daily or weekly meetings, others may only require monthly or quarterly gatherings.

Types of Meetings

Consider different types of meetings, including status updates, problem-solving sessions, and strategic planning meetings. Tailor the meeting format to the specific objectives.

Remote Meetings

With the increasing prevalence of remote work and multi-site operations, remote meetings have become essential. Ensure that remote meetings are just as effective as in-person meetings through proper preparation and technology.

Structuring Productive Team Meetings

Effective team meetings are the cornerstone of clear communication and efficient collaboration within a solar operations team. Let's explore the strategies and best practices for structuring productive team meetings that drive progress and foster a culture of excellence.

Setting the Meeting Objectives

Clearly Defined Goals

Every team meeting should have well-defined objectives. Begin by asking, "What do we aim to accomplish in this meeting?" This clarity ensures that the meeting stays focused and productive.

Prioritizing Agenda Items

Create an agenda that lists the topics to be discussed in order of priority. Allocate more time to critical issues and less to routine updates, ensuring that the most important matters receive adequate attention.

Time Constraints

Set time limits for each agenda item to prevent meetings from running over schedule. Stick to these limits to respect participants' time and maintain engagement.

Opening and Welcome

Start the meeting with a brief welcome and introduction. Acknowledge team members and create a positive and inclusive atmosphere.

Review of Previous Action Items

Begin by reviewing action items and progress made since the last meeting. This keeps team members accountable for their commitments and provides context for the current discussion.

Presentation and Discussion

The heart of the meeting is the presentation and discussion of agenda items. Encourage active participation, questions, and constructive debate.

Problem-Solving and Decision-Making

For meetings focused on problem-solving or decision-making, use structured processes like brainstorming or SWOT analysis to guide the discussion and reach a conclusion.

Action Items and Next Steps

Summarize key takeaways and action items at the end of each agenda item. Assign responsibilities and deadlines to ensure that outcomes are achieved.

Facilitation and Participation

Effective Facilitation

Appoint a meeting leader or facilitator responsible for guiding the meeting. A skilled facilitator keeps discussions on track, encourages participation, and manages time effectively.

Encourage Participation

Foster an environment where all team members feel comfortable contributing. Encourage quieter team members to share their thoughts and ideas. Avoid dominance by a few participants.

Constructive Feedback

Promote a culture of constructive feedback. Encourage team members to provide input, offer alternative perspectives, and challenge assumptions when necessary.

Ensuring Accountability and Follow-Up

Action Items and Responsibilities

Document action items, responsibilities, and deadlines during the meeting. Distribute these records promptly to ensure that everyone is aware of their commitments.

Follow-Up Meetings

Schedule follow-up meetings to track progress on action items and revisit unresolved issues. These meetings ensure that goals are achieved and prevent items from falling through the cracks.

Meeting Minutes

Assign someone to take meeting minutes, which capture key discussions, decisions, and action items. Distribute the minutes to all participants for reference and accountability.

Post-Meeting Evaluation

After each meeting, gather feedback from team members to assess its effectiveness. Use this feedback to make improvements in the structure and conduct of future meetings.

Evolving Agenda

As the needs and priorities of your solar operations team change, adapt the meeting agenda accordingly. Be flexible in responding to emerging challenges and opportunities.

By setting clear objectives, organizing meetings effectively, facilitating participation, and ensuring accountability, you can harness the full potential of your team's collective knowledge and expertise. Productive meetings lead to better decision-making, streamlined operations, and ultimately, the success of your solar energy projects.

Using Technology for Remote Collaboration

In today's interconnected world, remote collaboration is a key component of efficient solar operations management. Let's explore the role of technology in enabling effective remote collaboration within solar operations teams, whether they're spread across different locations or working from remote sites.

The Need for Remote Collaboration

Distributed Teams

Modern solar operations often involve teams working across multiple sites or remotely. This may include personnel responsible for different solar installations or those working from geographically dispersed locations.

Real-Time Information

Solar operations rely on real-time data and communication. To make informed decisions and respond to challenges promptly, team members need access to up-to-date information and the ability to communicate seamlessly.

Efficiency and Cost Savings

Remote collaboration technologies can significantly improve efficiency by reducing the need for travel and enabling teams to work together efficiently, regardless of location. This can result in cost savings and enhanced productivity.

Best Practices for Effective Remote Collaboration

Video Conferencing

Video conferencing platforms enable face-to-face communication and collaboration, even when team members are miles apart. They facilitate discussions, presentations, and problem-solving sessions.

Instant Messaging and Chat Apps

Instant messaging apps allow for quick and informal communication. They are useful for short updates, questions, and staying connected throughout the day.

Project Management Software

Project management tools help teams coordinate tasks, track progress, and manage timelines. They provide visibility into project status and promote accountability.

Cloud-Based Document Collaboration

Cloud storage and collaboration platforms enable team members to access, edit, and share documents in real-time. This ensures that everyone has access to the latest versions of important files.

Data Analytics and Monitoring Tools

For solar operations, data analytics and monitoring tools are invaluable. They provide insights into equipment performance, energy production, and maintenance needs, helping teams make informed decisions remotely.

Clear Communication

Emphasize the importance of clear and concise communication. Encourage team members to articulate their thoughts, ask questions, and summarize key points to ensure everyone is on the same page.

Set Expectations

Establish clear expectations for remote collaboration. Define roles, responsibilities, and communication protocols to minimize misunderstandings.

Regular Check-Ins

Schedule regular check-in meetings or status updates to keep the team connected. These meetings can be daily, weekly, or as needed, depending on the project's complexity.

Security Measures

Ensure that remote collaboration tools and platforms adhere to robust security standards. Protect sensitive data and communications from potential breaches.

Training and Support

Provide training and support to team members to ensure they are proficient in using remote collaboration tools. Offer assistance when technical issues arise.

Challenges and Solutions

Connectivity Issues

In some remote locations, internet connectivity may be unreliable. Consider satellite internet or offline modes for critical applications.

Time Zone Differences

When team members are spread across different time zones, schedule meetings at times that are convenient for all participants or rotate meeting times to ensure fairness.

Overcoming Isolation

Remote work can sometimes lead to feelings of isolation. Foster a sense of belonging through virtual team-building activities and regular social interactions.

Monitoring and Accountability

Use project management software and key performance indicators to monitor progress and hold team members accountable for their tasks and responsibilities.

Technology plays a pivotal role in enabling effective remote collaboration within solar operations teams. By leveraging the right tools and adopting best practices, teams can communicate seamlessly, access critical information, and work together efficiently, regardless of physical location. This approach not only enhances the productivity of solar operations but also contributes to a more flexible and agile workforce ready to tackle the challenges of the modern energy landscape.

[Chapter 4] - Managing Personnel Performance

Setting Clear Expectations and Goals

Effectively managing performance and setting clear expectations and goals are fundamental to achieving success in solar operations management. Let's dig into the strategies and practices that empower solar operations managers to drive high performance within their teams.

Goal Alignment

Setting clear expectations and goals aligns team members with the organization's mission and objectives. When everyone understands their role and what is expected of them, it fosters a sense of purpose and direction.

Performance Improvement

Clear expectations and goals provide a benchmark against which team members can measure their performance. They create a pathway for improvement and development.

Accountability

Setting expectations and goals creates a framework for accountability. Team members are more likely to take ownership of their responsibilities when they know what is expected of them.

Motivation

Well-defined goals provide motivation and a sense of accomplishment when they are achieved. They give team members something to strive for and a reason to put forth their best effort.

Setting Clear Expectations

Role Clarity

Ensure that each team member has a clear understanding of their role and responsibilities within the solar operations team. Document these responsibilities and communicate them effectively.

Performance Metrics

Define key performance indicators (KPIs) that align with team goals and organizational objectives. These metrics should be specific, measurable, achievable, relevant, and time-bound (SMART).

Communication of Expectations

Use regular one-on-one meetings, performance reviews, and team meetings to communicate and reinforce expectations. Encourage team members to ask questions and seek clarification when needed.

Setting Goals

Establishing Performance Goals

Performance goals should be directly tied to team and organizational objectives. They may include targets related to energy production, equipment uptime, safety records, and environmental sustainability.

Individual Development Goals

In addition to performance goals, encourage team members to set individual development goals. These goals can relate to skill acquisition, certifications, or career advancement within the organization.

Collaboration Goals

Promote collaboration within the team by setting goals that encourage teamwork, knowledge sharing, and mutual support.

Performance Management and Feedback

Regular Performance Reviews

Conduct regular performance reviews with team members to evaluate progress toward goals, provide feedback, and identify areas for improvement.

Constructive Feedback

Offer constructive feedback that is specific, actionable, and based on objective data. Focus on both strengths and areas for improvement.

Recognition and Rewards

Recognize and reward exceptional performance to motivate team members and reinforce a culture of excellence.

Addressing Performance Challenges

Early Intervention

Identify performance issues early and address them promptly. Provide additional support or training as needed to help team members overcome challenges.

Performance Improvement Plans

In cases of persistent performance challenges, develop performance improvement plans that outline specific actions, timelines, and support mechanisms to help team members succeed.

Termination

As a last resort, if performance issues continue and cannot be resolved, consider the possibility of termination. Ensure that this process is carried out fairly and in accordance with applicable employment laws.

Adaptation and Flexibility

Changing Goals and Objectives

In a dynamic field like solar operations, goals and objectives may need to be adjusted in response to changing circumstances or industry trends. Be adaptable and open to modifying goals as needed.

Continuous Improvement

Encourage a culture of continuous improvement within the team. Regularly review and assess goals and expectations to ensure they remain relevant and effective.

By providing a clear roadmap, offering regular feedback, and fostering a culture of accountability and continuous improvement, solar operations managers can lead their teams to consistently achieve high levels of performance and contribute to the overall success of large-scale solar energy projects.

Performance Evaluation and Feedback

Performance evaluation and feedback are essential components of effective solar operations management. Let's explore the processes and best practices that enable solar operations managers to assess team performance, provide constructive feedback, and drive continuous improvement.

Assessing Progress

Performance evaluations provide an opportunity to assess team and individual progress toward achieving goals and meeting expectations.

Identifying Strengths and Areas for Improvement

Through evaluation, strengths and areas for improvement become apparent, allowing for targeted development and support.

Feedback and Communication

Performance evaluations facilitate open and constructive communication between managers and team members. They provide a platform for discussing performance, expectations, and career development.

Decision-Making

Evaluation results may influence decisions related to promotions, raises, training, and even staffing changes when necessary.

Preparing for Performance Evaluations

Clear Performance Metrics

Establish clear and measurable performance metrics and goals from the outset, ensuring that team members understand how their performance will be evaluated.

Documentation

Maintain records of team members' accomplishments, contributions, and performance-related incidents throughout the evaluation period.

Self-Assessment

Encourage team members to conduct self-assessments. This process allows them to reflect on their performance, strengths, and areas for improvement.

Performance Review Forms

Create standardized performance review forms that encompass the relevant evaluation criteria, metrics, and space for comments.

Conducting Performance Evaluations

Scheduled Meetings

Schedule performance evaluation meetings well in advance to allow both managers and team members time to prepare.

Constructive Feedback

Provide balanced feedback that includes praise for achievements and constructive criticism for areas that require improvement.

Open Dialogue

Create a two-way dialogue during performance evaluations, allowing team members to share their perspectives, concerns, and career aspirations.

Goal Setting

Work collaboratively with team members to set new performance goals and expectations for the next evaluation period.

Giving Constructive Feedback

Specificity

Offer specific examples and data to support feedback. Vague or general feedback is less actionable.

Timeliness

Provide feedback promptly, especially when addressing performance issues. Timely feedback allows for prompt corrective action.

Focus on Behavior

Base feedback on observed behavior rather than making personal judgments or assumptions about a team member's character.

Balance Positive and Negative Feedback

Acknowledge accomplishments and strengths alongside areas that need improvement. A balanced approach encourages motivation and growth.

Handling Performance Challenges

Performance Improvement Plans

For team members facing persistent performance challenges, develop performance improvement plans (PIPs) that outline specific actions, support mechanisms, and timelines for improvement.

Development Opportunities

Identify opportunities for training, mentoring, or skill development to address performance gaps.

Termination as a Last Resort

If performance issues cannot be resolved, consider the possibility of termination as a last resort, ensuring it complies with applicable employment laws and is handled fairly and professionally.

Continuous Feedback and Development

Ongoing Feedback

Performance evaluation should not be a once-a-year event. Encourage continuous feedback and communication throughout the year to address issues promptly and provide recognition for ongoing achievements.

Career Development

Discuss career development and growth opportunities during performance evaluations. Provide guidance on potential career paths within the organization.

Feedback on the Evaluation Process

Seek feedback from team members on the evaluation process itself. Use their input to make improvements and ensure the process remains effective and fair.

Performance evaluation and feedback are indispensable tools for managing and improving the performance of a solar operations team. By establishing clear metrics, conducting regular evaluations, providing constructive feedback, and fostering a culture of continuous development, solar operations managers can empower their teams to excel in their roles and future careers.

Addressing Challenges and Conflicts

Challenges and conflicts are an inevitable part of managing a solar operations team. Let's dig into strategies and best practices for identifying, addressing, and resolving challenges and conflicts to ensure the smooth operation of large-scale solar assets.

Recognizing Challenges and Conflicts

Equipment Failures

Solar operations can face unexpected equipment failures, which may disrupt energy production and require immediate attention.

Environmental Factors

Weather-related challenges, such as extreme heat or storms, can impact solar operations, affecting both equipment and personnel.

Resource Limitations

Resource constraints, including budget limitations and staffing shortages, can present operational challenges.

Interpersonal Conflicts

Team members may experience conflicts related to differences in communication styles, work approaches, or personal issues.

Conflict Resolution Strategies

Open Communication

Encourage open and honest communication among team members. Create a safe space for discussing concerns and conflicts.

Active Listening

Ensure that individuals involved in conflicts actively listen to one another. Encourage empathy and understanding of different perspectives.

Mediation

In cases of interpersonal conflicts, consider involving a neutral third party as a mediator to facilitate resolution.

Problem-Solving and Decision-Making

Root Cause Analysis

When faced with challenges, conduct thorough root cause analyses to identify the underlying issues. This process helps prevent recurring problems.

Collaborative Problem-Solving

Encourage team members to work collaboratively in solving challenges. Diverse perspectives often lead to more innovative and effective solutions.

Data-Driven Decisions

Base decisions on data and evidence whenever possible. This approach fosters objectivity and minimizes subjective biases.

Handling Major Equipment Failures

Emergency Response Plans

Develop and maintain emergency response plans that outline procedures for addressing major equipment failures. Ensure all team members are familiar with these plans.

Rapid Response Teams

Designate specialized teams or personnel trained to respond swiftly to equipment failures. This proactive approach can minimize downtime and mitigate damage.

Vendor Relationships

Cultivate strong relationships with equipment vendors. Prompt vendor support and maintenance can be crucial in resolving major failures.

Resilience and Adaptability

Scenario Planning

Conduct scenario planning exercises to prepare for potential challenges and develop strategies for addressing them proactively.

Continuous Improvement

Implement a culture of continuous improvement. Regularly review past challenges and conflicts to identify areas where processes or procedures can be refined.

Communication with Stakeholders

Transparent Communication

Maintain transparent communication with stakeholders, including investors, regulators, and local communities, about challenges and their resolutions.

Mitigating Impact

Explain the steps taken to mitigate the impact of challenges and conflicts on energy production, safety, and the environment.

Engaging Stakeholders

Engage stakeholders in the resolution process when appropriate, seeking their input and support.

Addressing challenges and conflicts is a crucial aspect of managing solar operations effectively. By promoting open communication, implementing conflict resolution strategies, and fostering a culture of adaptability and continuous improvement, solar operations managers can navigate challenges successfully, maintain high levels of performance, and ensure the continued success of large-scale solar projects.

[Chapter 5] - Managing Site Performance

Site Orientation

The site orientation for a solar site is an important aspect of ensuring optimal performance, safety, and ease of maintenance. A comprehensive safety site orientation should cover various aspects to ensure the well-being of all personnel on-site. Here are key elements to include:

1. Introduction to the Site:

- Provide an overview of the solar site, including its purpose, layout, and potential hazards.

- Identify key personnel responsible for safety and emergency response.

2. Emergency Procedures:

- Clearly outline emergency evacuation procedures, including assembly points.

- Provide information on how to report emergencies or incidents.

- Explain the location and use of emergency equipment, such as fire extinguishers, first aid kits, and emergency exits.

3. Personal Protective Equipment (PPE):

- Specify the required PPE for the site. This may include hard hats, safety glasses, gloves, steel-toed boots, and high-visibility clothing.

- Demonstrate the correct way to wear and use each type of PPE.

4. Site Access and Restricted Areas:

- Define authorized access points and areas that are off-limits.

- Clearly mark restricted zones and explain the reasons for restricted access.

5. Hazardous Materials and Substances:

- Identify any hazardous materials or substances present on-site.

- Provide information on Material Safety Data Sheets (MSDS) and safe handling procedures.

6. Electrical Safety:

- Emphasize the importance of following electrical safety protocols.

- Identify high-voltage areas and explain safety measures when working with electrical equipment.

7. Fire Safety:

- Explain the location of fire exits and firefighting equipment.

- Provide guidance on responding to fire emergencies and the use of fire suppression equipment.

8. Environmental Considerations:

- Address environmental hazards, such as extreme temperatures, weather conditions, or any potential impact on local ecosystems.

9. Equipment Operation and Procedures:

- Provide instructions for the safe operation of specific equipment on-site.

- Emphasize the importance of following manufacturer guidelines and procedures.

10. Communication Protocols:

- Establish communication channels and protocols for reporting incidents, hazards, or safety concerns.

- Ensure that all personnel are aware of how to communicate effectively during normal operations and emergencies.

11. Health and Hygiene:

- Provide information on facilities available for personal hygiene.

- Discuss any health considerations related to the site, such as exposure to noise or air quality concerns.

12. Training Requirements:

- Identify any specific training requirements for individuals working on or visiting the site.

- Ensure that everyone is aware of their training status and any additional training needed.

Conducting a thorough safety site orientation is essential to create a culture of safety and ensure that all individuals on-site are well-prepared to handle potential risks and emergencies. Regular updates and refresher sessions should also be conducted to keep everyone informed about changes to site conditions or procedures.

Maximizing Solar Asset Efficiency

Efficient site performance is vital for the success of solar energy projects. Let's explore the strategies and best practices that solar operations managers can employ to optimize solar asset efficiency and ensure that energy production remains at peak levels.

The Significance of Monitoring and Analytics

Monitoring and analytics play a pivotal role in maximizing the efficiency and performance of solar energy assets. I Let's dig into the strategies and best practices that solar operations managers can employ to harness data-driven insights for performance optimization.

Data-Driven Decision Making

Monitoring and analytics provide valuable data and insights that empower data-driven decision-making, enhancing the overall efficiency of solar operations.

Early Issue Detection

Continuous monitoring allows for the early detection of issues or deviations in performance, enabling prompt corrective action.

Performance Benchmarking

Analytics enable performance benchmarking against industry standards and similar installations, revealing opportunities for improvement.

Efficiency Gains

Efficient use of data can lead to improvements in energy production, cost savings, and overall asset performance.

Performance Analytics

Performance Ratios

Calculate performance ratios (PR) and capacity factors to assess how effectively solar assets convert sunlight into electricity.

Predictive Analytics

Utilize predictive analytics to forecast energy production, equipment maintenance needs, and potential system failures.

Anomaly Detection

Implement anomaly detection algorithms that automatically flag irregularities in performance data, allowing for swift investigation and resolution.

Historical Data Analysis

Analyze historical data to identify long-term trends, seasonal variations, and areas where system improvements can be made.

Availability Calculations

Solar site availability refers to the percentage of time that a solar power system is operational and able to generate electricity. The availability of a solar site is a crucial factor in determining the overall efficiency and economic viability of a solar power project. The calculation of solar site availability involves assessing the uptime and downtime of the solar power system. Here's a general outline of how solar site availability is calculated:

Downtime Definition:

Downtime includes any period during which the solar power system is not generating electricity. This can be due to scheduled maintenance, unscheduled maintenance (repairs), or unexpected system failures.

Uptime Calculation:

Uptime is the opposite of downtime and represents the period when the solar power system is operational and generating electricity. It is typically expressed as a percentage of the total time.

$$Availability \% = \left(\frac{Total\ Operational\ Time}{Total\ Time}\right) \times 100$$

Availability Calculation:

Availability is then calculated by subtracting the downtime percentage from 100%.

$$Availability \% = 100\% - Downtime \%$$

Downtime Identification:

Downtime can be categorized as scheduled or unscheduled. Scheduled downtime is planned in advance for routine maintenance activities, while unscheduled downtime is unexpected and occurs due to equipment failures or other unforeseen issues.

This calculation and the downtime "carve-outs" (or exemptions) can vary based on contract or company.

It's important to note that site availability is just one aspect of overall solar project performance, but is generally one of the contractual obligations for service providers. Factors such as solar resource availability, system design, and operational and maintenance practices also play crucial roles in determining the success of a solar power project.

Asset Health Monitoring

Condition Monitoring

Implement condition monitoring systems that continuously assess the health of critical equipment, such as inverters and transformers.

Predictive Maintenance

Leverage asset health data to predict maintenance needs and optimize maintenance schedules, reducing downtime and maintenance costs.

Failure Mode Analysis

Conduct failure mode analysis to understand the root causes of equipment failures and develop strategies to prevent them.

Performance Monitoring

Monitoring and analytics are indispensable tools for solar operations managers aiming to optimize the performance of their solar assets. By implementing robust monitoring systems, leveraging data analytics for insights, and continuously reviewing and adapting strategies, solar operations managers can enhance energy production, minimize downtime, and ensure the long-term success of their solar energy projects. Here's how you can monitor the performance of a solar PV utility site:

Data Acquisition System (DAS):

Install a robust data acquisition system that collects real-time data from various components of the solar PV system. The DAS should capture data from solar panels, inverters, weather stations, and other relevant sensors.

SCADA (Supervisory Control and Data Acquisition):

Implement a SCADA system to remotely monitor and control the solar PV plant. SCADA provides real-time visualization and control capabilities, enabling operators to monitor the entire plant from a centralized location.

Inverter Monitoring:

Monitor the performance of individual inverters and track their efficiency, power output, and any error or fault codes. Inverters play a crucial role in converting DC power from solar panels to AC power for the grid, so monitoring their performance is essential.

Weather Monitoring:

Integrate weather monitoring stations to gather data on solar irradiance, ambient temperature, wind speed, and other weather parameters. Weather data helps correlate energy generation with external conditions and identify any weather-related issues.

Remote Sensing Technologies:

Use remote sensing technologies, such as drones or aerial imagery, to conduct inspections of the solar panels and identify potential defects or soiling.

Data Analytics and Reporting:

Utilize data analytics tools to analyze historical performance data and identify trends, anomalies, or areas that need improvement. Generate regular performance reports for management and stakeholders.

Alarm and Alert Systems:

Set up alarm and alert systems that trigger notifications when certain performance parameters deviate from expected values or when errors occur in the system.

Irradiance Forecasting:

Use solar irradiance forecasting models to predict energy generation based on weather forecasts. This can aid in better grid integration and planning.

Maintenance Management:

Integrate the monitoring system with a maintenance management platform to schedule and track maintenance tasks, ensuring timely servicing and reducing downtime.

Performance Benchmarking:

Benchmark the solar PV plant's performance against similar systems or industry standards to identify areas for improvement and optimization.

Cybersecurity Measures:

Implement robust cybersecurity measures to protect the monitoring and control systems from potential cyber threats.

Proper monitoring and analysis of the solar PV utility site's performance help optimize energy production, detect faults or underperforming components early, and ensure the plant operates at its full potential throughout its lifecycle.

Solar Underperformance

Solar underperformance can be caused by various factors, and identifying the specific cause requires careful analysis. Some typical causes of solar underperformance include:

Operation and Maintenance (O&M) Negligence:

Lack of regular maintenance and timely repairs can lead to underperformance over time.

Faulty Inverters:

Inverters are crucial components that convert DC power from solar panels to AC power for use. Faulty inverters or inverter malfunctions can reduce system performance.

Wiring Issues:

Poorly connected or damaged wiring can lead to power losses and decreased system efficiency.

Ground Faults and Short Circuits:

Ground faults and short circuits can occur due to damaged insulation or faulty electrical connections, leading to system malfunctions or shutdowns.

Electrical Surges:

Electrical surges caused by lightning strikes or utility grid fluctuations can damage the system's electronic components.

Tracking Errors:

For tracking systems that follow the sun's movement, errors in tracking alignment can result in reduced energy capture.

Weather Variability:

Weather fluctuations, including cloud cover and temperature changes, can impact solar energy production on a day-to-day basis.

Dirt, Dust, and Debris:

Accumulation of dirt, dust, bird droppings, and other debris on solar panels can reduce sunlight absorption and hinder energy generation. Bird droppings can accumulate on panels and reduce energy generation.

Shading:

Shading from nearby trees, buildings, or other obstructions can significantly impact the performance of solar panels by reducing the amount of sunlight they receive.

Module Degradation:

Over time, solar panels may experience degradation due to exposure to harsh weather conditions, which can lead to a decrease in efficiency.

Module Mismatch:

If the solar panels in an array are not well-matched in terms of electrical characteristics, it can lead to energy losses.

PID (Potential Induced Degradation):

PID can cause power loss in solar panels due to voltage differences between the cells and the grounded frame. It typically occurs in humid environments.

Inaccurate Irradiance Measurements:

Improperly calibrated irradiance sensors can result in inaccurate measurements, affecting system performance calculations.

Inverter Clipping:

In some cases, inverters may reach their maximum power output capacity, leading to clipping of energy production during peak periods.

Corrosion and Moisture:

Exposure to moisture, salt, or other corrosive elements can damage the electrical connections and components, reducing the system's efficiency and lifespan.

System Age:

Older solar systems may experience wear and tear, reducing efficiency compared to newer installations.

Inadequate Design or Installation:

Improper system design or installation can lead to suboptimal performance, premature wear, and system failures.

To address underperformance, periodic monitoring, thorough inspections, and prompt maintenance are essential. It is crucial to work with qualified technicians and experts to diagnose and rectify issues promptly to ensure the solar system operates at its optimal capacity. Additionally, implementing preventive maintenance practices and using performance monitoring tools can help prevent underperformance and prolong the lifespan of the solar installation.

Optimize Solar Asset Performance

To optimize solar asset performance, you can implement the following strategies:

O&M Best Practices:

Establish best practices for operations and maintenance (O&M) activities to ensure consistency and quality in managing the solar assets.

Professional Training and Development:

Train and educate personnel on the latest solar technologies, maintenance practices, and safety protocols to enhance their skills and knowledge.

Regular Documentation

Maintain comprehensive records of maintenance activities, inspections, and equipment performance. This documentation is valuable for tracking changes over time and for warranty claims.

Performance-Based Contracts:

Use performance-based contracts with O&M service providers to incentivize them to achieve optimal system performance.

Performance Monitoring:

Utilize monitoring systems to track the performance of individual panels and the entire solar array. Analyze data to identify underperforming panels or system issues.

Real-Time Performance Monitoring:

Use real-time performance monitoring tools to detect performance deviations and take corrective actions quickly.

Fault Detection and Diagnostics:

Implement fault detection and diagnostic systems to identify and resolve issues promptly. This helps prevent prolonged downtime and ensures maximum energy generation.

Regular Maintenance and Cleaning:

Develop a comprehensive maintenance schedule to inspect and clean solar panels, inverters, and other components. Regular maintenance ensures optimal system performance and longevity.

Weather Forecasting and Response:

Monitor weather forecasts to anticipate changes in solar irradiance or weather conditions. Adjust system operations or curtailment strategies accordingly.

Predictive Analytics:

Utilize predictive analytics to forecast solar generation, demand patterns, and potential system issues. This helps optimize energy dispatch and system performance.

System Upgrades and Retrofits:

Consider upgrading or retrofitting older solar panels or components with more efficient and advanced technologies to improve overall performance.

Environmental Considerations:

Consider the environmental impact of solar installations, such as the potential for soiling or dust accumulation, and implement appropriate mitigation measures.

By implementing these optimization strategies, solar asset owners can maximize energy generation, reduce operational costs, and improve the overall profitability and sustainability of their solar facilities.

Maintenance Guidance

Routine maintenance and preventive measures are essential to ensure the longevity and optimal performance of solar energy assets.

Here are some maintenance best practices:

Preventive Measures

Training and Certification

Ensure that maintenance personnel are well-trained and certified in the safe and effective maintenance of solar equipment.

Safety Inspections:

Conduct safety inspections regularly to ensure compliance with safety standards and prevent accidents during maintenance activities.

Visual Inspections:

Regularly inspect the entire solar array for signs of physical damage, loose connections, and worn-out components. Catching these issues early can prevent more extensive damage and downtime.

Torque Checks:

Perform a torque check on the mounting structure and all electrical connections to ensure they are properly secured. Proper torque helps prevent loosening over time.

Inverter Maintenance:

Inverters are critical components of a solar PV system. Follow the manufacturer's guidelines for maintenance, including routine checks, cleaning, and servicing.

Vegetation Management:

Keep vegetation around the solar panels under control. Overgrown vegetation can create safety issues, wildfire risks, or cast shadows on the panels and reduce energy production. This can be one of the most expensive O&M budget items.

Monitoring System:

Implement a comprehensive monitoring system that tracks the performance of individual panels and the overall system. This enables early detection of any anomalies and allows for proactive maintenance.

Data Analysis:

Analyze the performance data regularly to identify trends and potential issues. This data-driven approach can help optimize the system's performance and identify areas for improvement.

Firmware Updates

Stay up to date with firmware and software updates for inverters and monitoring systems. These updates often include performance improvements and bug fixes.

Regular Cleaning:

Dust, dirt, bird droppings, and other debris can accumulate on the solar panels, reducing their efficiency. Regularly clean the panels with water, soft brushes, or automated cleaning systems, especially in dusty or polluted environments.

Infrared Scanning:

Conduct periodic infrared (IR) scans to identify hot spots in the solar panels, combiner boxes, inverters Hot spots can indicate defects or malfunctioning cells and addressing them promptly can prevent further damage.

Extreme Weather Precautions:

Prepare for extreme weather events like storms, hurricanes, and heavy snowfall. Reinforce the mounting structures and take preventive measures to avoid damage during severe weather.

Spare Parts Inventory:

Maintain an inventory of critical spare parts to minimize downtime in case of component failures.

Regular Performance Testing:

Periodically test the system's performance against its expected output to detect any deviations and take corrective action.

Pest Control:

Ensure that the solar installation is protected against rodents and other pests that might damage the system's wiring or components.

Partnering with Experts:

Consider partnering with experienced solar O&M companies that specialize in utility-scale installations. Their expertise and resources can enhance the efficiency of maintenance practices.

Work Optimization

The best work management practices ensure that tasks are planned, executed, and monitored efficiently to achieve the desired outcomes. Here are some key work management practices that can lead to increased productivity and effectiveness:

Effective Planning:

Properly plan tasks, projects, or maintenance activities in advance. Clearly define objectives, scope, and deadlines, and allocate necessary resources.

Clear Communication:

Establish effective communication channels to ensure all team members are on the same page. Regularly update stakeholders on progress and address any issues promptly.

Task Prioritization:

Prioritize tasks based on urgency, importance, and impact on overall goals. Focus on high-priority items to ensure efficient use of time and resources.

Standard Operating Procedures (SOPs):

Develop and follow standardized procedures for recurring tasks. SOPs streamline work processes and maintain consistency.

Resource Allocation:

Allocate resources appropriately based on workload and requirements. Ensure that team members have the necessary tools and equipment to perform their tasks effectively.

Task Delegation:

Delegate tasks to the right individuals based on their expertise and workload capacity. Avoid micromanagement and foster a sense of responsibility among team members.

Work Tracking and Reporting:

Use project management tools or software to track progress and generate reports. Regularly review performance metrics to identify areas for improvement.

Risk Management:

Identify potential risks and develop mitigation strategies. Anticipate challenges and have contingency plans in place to handle unforeseen issues.

Work-Life Balance:

Encourage work-life balance to prevent burnout and maintain employee morale and productivity.

Adaptability:

Be flexible and adapt to changing circumstances or project requirements. Embrace innovation and new technologies to stay ahead in the industry.

By implementing these best work management practices, organizations can optimize their operations, increase efficiency, and deliver high-quality products or services to their customers.

Energization

Energizing a utility-scale solar site involves the process of bringing the system online and connecting it to the grid. Here's an overview of the typical steps involved in energizing a utility-scale site:

1. Preparation and Safety Checks:

 - Ensure that all personnel involved are equipped with appropriate personal protective equipment (PPE) and are aware of safety protocols.

 - Verify that the solar site components, including PV modules, inverters, and controls, are installed, tested, and functioning properly.

2. Grid Connection and Interconnection:

 - Coordinate with grid operators and utility personnel to establish the necessary interconnection points and permissions to connect the solar site to the grid.

3. Electrical Testing:

 - Perform electrical testing to verify that the components are properly wired, grounded, and connected according to design specifications.

 - Verify that the grid connection is compliant with local codes and standards.

4. Commissioning and Testing:

 - Commission the solar site by configuring its control systems, parameters, and communication interfaces.

 - Test the communication between the solar site and the grid management system to ensure that commands and signals are transmitted accurately.

6. System Verification and Functional Testing:

 - Test the solar site under different operational scenarios, such as charging, discharging, and grid stabilization.

 - Verify that the solar site operates as intended, responding to changes in grid conditions and delivering energy as required.

7. Safety Checks and Alarms Testing:

- Test safety systems, alarms, and emergency shutdown procedures to ensure that they function correctly.

- Verify that alarms are triggered appropriately for abnormal conditions.

8. Regulatory Compliance:

- Ensure that the solar site complies with all local regulations, codes, and standards governing utility-scale energy storage systems.

9. Grid Integration Testing:

- Test the solar site's ability to provide grid services, such as frequency regulation, voltage support, and peak shaving.

- Verify that the solar site can respond accurately and quickly to grid signals.

10. Grid Interaction and Synchronization:

- Synchronize the solar site with the grid by matching its frequency and voltage levels to the grid's requirements.

- Test the solar site's ability to smoothly transition between grid-connected and islanded operation (if applicable).

11. Performance Monitoring:

- Implement performance monitoring systems to track the solar site's operations, energy flows, and grid interactions.

12. Initial Operation and Fine-Tuning:

- Begin initial operation of the solar site by providing grid services, load shifting, or other services as intended.

- Fine-tune control parameters and strategies based on operational data and feedback.

13. Operational Handover and Documentation:

- Provide training to operators and maintenance personnel on the solar site's operation, controls, and maintenance procedures.

- Document the system configuration, control settings, testing results, and safety protocols.

14. Ongoing Monitoring and Maintenance:

- Continuously monitor the solar site's performance, addressing any anomalies or issues promptly.

- Schedule regular maintenance to ensure the solar site's reliability and optimal performance.

The specific steps for energizing a utility-scale solar site may vary based on the technology used, the solar site manufacturer's recommendations, regulatory requirements, and local grid conditions. It's crucial to work closely with qualified professionals and follow established procedures to ensure a safe and successful energization process.

Construction to Operations Turnover

When transitioning a utility-scale solar site from construction and commissioning to operational use, several key turnover items need to be addressed. These items ensure a smooth handover, effective operation, and ongoing maintenance. Here are some important turnover items to consider:

1. As-Built Drawings and Documentation:

    - Provide accurate and up to date as-built drawings, schematics, and technical documentation that reflect the actual configuration of the solar site after construction and commissioning.

2. Operation and Maintenance Manuals:

    - Deliver comprehensive operation and maintenance manuals that provide detailed instructions for operating the solar site, performing routine maintenance, troubleshooting, and addressing common issues.

3. Training Materials:

    - Develop training materials and conduct training sessions for operators, maintenance personnel, and other relevant staff members.

4. System Configuration and Settings:

    - Document the site's configuration, settings, and parameters used for different operational scenarios.

    - Provide clear instructions for adjusting or fine-tuning control settings when necessary.

5. Testing and Commissioning Reports:

    - Compile detailed reports on the testing and commissioning processes, including the results of various tests, system performance data, and any adjustments made.

6. Performance Baseline Data:

    - Provide baseline data captured during commissioning to serve as a reference for future performance evaluations.

    - Include data on energy efficiency, power output, PV capacity, and other key performance metrics.

7. Spare Parts Inventory:

- Create an inventory of critical spare parts and components that might be needed for maintenance or repairs.

8. Warranties and Service Agreements:

- Ensure that all warranties, service agreements, and maintenance contracts are transferred to the new owner or operator.

- Clearly outline the terms and conditions of these agreements.

9. Safety Procedures and Protocols:

- Document safety procedures, protocols, and emergency response plan specific to the solar site.

- Include instructions for handling hazardous materials, addressing fires, and responding to other safety incidents.

10. Regulatory Compliance and Permits:

- Provide documentation that demonstrates compliance with local regulations, permits, and codes related to the solar site's construction, operation, and safety.

11. Data Logging and Reporting Systems:

- Set up data logging and reporting systems that provide real-time information on the solar site's performance, energy flows, and grid interactions.

- Ensure that the systems are accessible and user-friendly for operators.

12. Communication and Monitoring Systems:

- Document communication protocols and interfaces used for monitoring and controlling the solar site.

- Provide access credentials and guidelines for remote monitoring and management.

13. Ongoing Support Contacts:

- Share contact information for technical support and troubleshooting, including manufacturer contacts or service providers.

14. Handover Meetings and Discussions:

- Conduct handover meetings with key stakeholders, including project managers, operators, and maintenance personnel.

- Address any questions, concerns, or special considerations related to the solar site's operation.

15. Transition Plan and Timeline:

- Outline a transition plan that describes the steps involved in handing over the solar site from construction to operation.

- Include a timeline for each phase and milestone.

16. Lessons Learned and Improvement Recommendations:

- Summarize lessons learned during the construction and commissioning phases and provide recommendations for improving future projects.

By addressing these key turnover items, you can ensure a successful transition from the construction and commissioning phase to the operational phase of a utility-scale solar system. Effective documentation, training, and communication are essential to maximizing the system's performance, safety, and longevity.

Emergency Response and Repairs

Emergency Protocols

Develop emergency response protocols to address unforeseen equipment failures or incidents. Ensure that team members are well-prepared to act swiftly in case of emergencies.

Emergency Action Plan (EAP) / Emergency Response Plan (ERP)

Emergency action plans (EAPs), sometimes referred to as Emergency response plans (ERP) for solar facilities are essential to ensure the safety of personnel, the public, and the environment during unexpected events or emergencies. Here are key considerations and information that should be included in an emergency action plan for a solar facility:

1. Emergency Contacts and Communication: Provide a list of emergency contact numbers for local authorities, emergency services, facility management, and key personnel. Outline communication protocols for alerting staff, contractors, and relevant stakeholders during emergencies.

2. Evacuation Procedures: Detail evacuation routes, assembly points, and procedures for evacuating personnel and visitors from different areas of the solar facility. Include information on how to assist individuals with disabilities or specific needs during evacuations.

3. Emergency Shutdown Procedures: Describe the process for shutting down combiner boxes, inverters, and other critical systems in the event of an emergency. Include instructions for isolating electrical power and ensuring the safety of personnel and responders.

4. Fire Safety: Outline fire prevention measures, firefighting equipment locations, and procedures for dealing with fires. Highlight the risks associated with solar panels and electrical equipment in firefighting efforts.

5. Medical Emergencies: Provide guidance on responding to medical emergencies, including first aid procedures, the location of first aid kits, and the availability of trained personnel or medical professionals on-site.

6. Severe Weather and Natural Disasters: Describe procedures for responding to severe weather events (such as storms, hurricanes, or tornadoes) and natural disasters (earthquakes, floods). Identify safe areas or shelters and detail how personnel will be informed and protected.

7. Hazardous Materials and Chemicals: If applicable, provide information about any hazardous materials or chemicals on-site, their storage locations, handling procedures, and protocols for containing spills or leaks.

8. Security Threats: Address potential security threats, such as unauthorized access, vandalism, or terrorism. Include measures for securing the facility and reporting suspicious activities.

9. Training and Drills: Specify the frequency and types of emergency response training and drills that personnel should undergo. Conduct regular drills to ensure that all staff are familiar with the procedures and can respond effectively.

10. Notification and Reporting: Detail the process for reporting emergencies, incidents, or potential hazards to appropriate authorities, management, and regulatory agencies.

11. Documentation and Record-Keeping: Outline procedures for documenting and reporting emergency actions, including incident reports, lessons learned, and any required regulatory reporting.

12. Review and Updates: Emphasize the importance of regularly reviewing and updating the emergency action plan to incorporate new risks, changes in regulations, or improvements in emergency response procedures.

13. Public and Community Outreach: Consider strategies for communicating emergency procedures to neighboring communities, residents, and relevant stakeholders to promote public safety and awareness.

14. Coordination with Local Authorities: Establish a relationship with local emergency response agencies and authorities to ensure effective collaboration and a coordinated response during emergencies.

15. Resources and Equipment: Provide information about the availability and locations of emergency equipment, such as fire extinguishers, first aid kits, emergency lighting, and communication devices.

Regular training, drills, and updates will help ensure that all staff members are prepared to respond appropriately during critical situations.

Spill, Prevention, Controls, and Countermeasures (SPCC)

An SPCC (Spill Prevention, Control, and Countermeasure) plan is a regulatory requirement established by the United States Environmental Protection Agency (EPA) under the Clean Water Act. It is designed to prevent oil spills and ensure the proper management of oil storage and handling to protect water resources, including navigable waters and adjoining shorelines. While SPCC plans are often associated with facilities that handle significant amounts of oil, they may also apply to certain aspects of a solar facility that involve oil storage or handling.

In the context of a solar facility, an SPCC plan might be required if the facility uses oil-filled equipment, such as transformers, inverters, or other components that contain dielectric oil or other types of oils. These oils have the potential to cause environmental harm if they were to spill or leak into water bodies or the environment.

An SPCC plan for a solar facility typically includes the following components:

1. Facility Description: Detailed information about the solar facility, its location, operations, and oil-handling activities and chemical composition of batteries.

2. Potential Oil Sources: Identification of all oil storage and handling areas within the facility, including transformers, inverters, storage tanks, and other equipment containing oil.

3. Spill Prevention Measures: Description of measures taken to prevent oil and chemical spills, including engineering controls, staff training, operating procedures, and maintenance practices.

4. Control Measures: Explanation of containment measures in place to prevent oil or battery chemicals from reaching navigable waters or adjoining shorelines in case of a spill. This may involve the use of secondary containment, dikes, berms, or other strategies.

5. Inspection and Maintenance: Details about regular inspection and maintenance activities, schedules, and records to ensure the continued effectiveness of spill prevention measures.

6. Reporting Procedures: Steps to follow in the event of an oil or chemical spill, including immediate notification to appropriate authorities and the implementation of response actions to minimize environmental damage.

7. Emergency Response: Plans for responding to spills, including personnel responsibilities, resources, and communication procedures.

8. Recordkeeping: Requirements for maintaining records related to SPCC plan implementation, inspections, maintenance, and spill response actions.

9. Professional Engineer Certification: Some facilities may require a certified Professional Engineer (PE) to review and certify the SPCC plan, especially if the facility has a large oil storage capacity.

It's important to note that the specific requirements of an SPCC plan can vary based on the facility.

Developing a Robust Maintenance Plan

A well-structured maintenance plan is essential for ensuring the reliability, performance, and longevity of solar energy assets. Let's dig into the strategies and best practices that solar operations managers can employ to develop a robust maintenance plan.

The Significance of a Maintenance Plan

Asset Reliability

A maintenance plan is crucial for ensuring the ongoing reliability of solar equipment and preventing unexpected breakdowns.

Energy Production

Effective maintenance directly impacts energy production levels, helping to maximize the return on investment (ROI) for solar projects.

Cost Control

Proactive maintenance reduces the overall cost of ownership by minimizing emergency repairs and downtime.

Safety

Maintenance plans include safety protocols and inspections that help mitigate safety risks for both personnel and the environment.

Components of a Maintenance Plan

Maintenance Scheduling

Develop a detailed schedule for routine inspections, preventive maintenance, and equipment servicing.

It is best practice to identify the seasonal adjustments that can significantly impact production. Inverter inspection, and filter and cooling system maintenance prior t to hot summer months can prevent overheating and derating or failures.

Each night there is an "outage" when the sun goes down, so maximizing site production but scheduling major work or maintenance at night when appropriate is effective.

Task Assignment

Clearly define roles and responsibilities for maintenance tasks, specifying who is responsible for each activity.

Spare Parts Management

Establish a spare parts inventory and procurement process to ensure timely availability of critical components.

Documentation

Maintain thorough documentation of maintenance activities, including inspection reports, service records, and equipment histories.

Data Analytics

Leverage data analytics and sensor data to predict equipment failures and performance issues.

Emergency Response

Emergency Protocols

Develop and communicate clear emergency response protocols to address equipment failures, accidents, and safety incidents.

Spare Parts Availability

Ensure that critical spare parts are readily available for prompt replacement during emergencies.

Asset Inventory

Create a comprehensive inventory of all equipment, including solar modules, inverters, trackers, cabling, and monitoring systems.

Vendor Relationships

Establish relationships with equipment vendors and service providers who can offer timely support during critical situations.

Environmental and Safety Considerations

Environmental Compliance

Ensure that maintenance practices align with environmental regulations, including waste disposal and hazardous material handling.

Safety Protocols

Develop and enforce safety protocols for maintenance activities to protect personnel and the environment.

Performance Evaluation and Continuous Improvement

Performance Metrics

Define key performance indicators (KPIs) to measure the effectiveness of the maintenance plan, such as equipment availability, mean time to repair (MTTR), and mean time between failures (MTBF).

MTBF (Mean Time Between Failures): MTBF is a measure of the average time a system or component operates between failures. It is a reliability indicator that reflects the system's robustness and stability. A higher MTBF suggests a more reliable system with fewer breakdowns.

MTTR (Mean Time To Repair): MTTR represents the average time it takes to repair a failed system or component and restore it to operational status. A lower MTTR implies quicker recovery and reduced downtime.

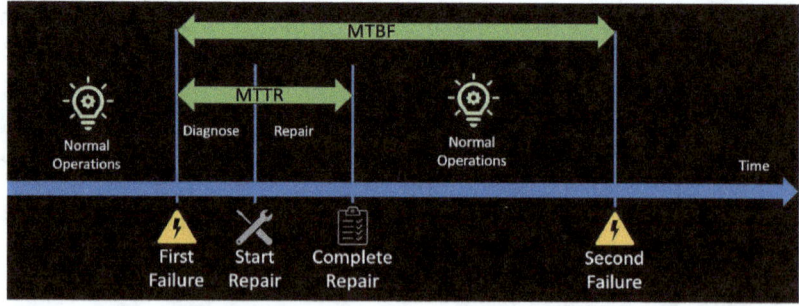

Root Cause Analysis

Conduct root cause analyses for equipment failures to identify systemic issues and implement corrective actions.

Training and Skill Development

Invest in training and skill development for maintenance personnel to ensure their competency and safety.

A robust maintenance plan is critical to the successful operation of solar energy assets. By creating a comprehensive plan that includes preventive and predictive maintenance, emergency response protocols, environmental considerations, and performance evaluation, solar operations managers can ensure the reliability and performance of their solar installations while minimizing downtime and costs.

Routine maintenance and preventive measures are essential to the long-term success of solar energy assets. By implementing a well-structured maintenance plan, conducting regular inspections, addressing issues promptly, and staying proactive in equipment upkeep, solar operations managers can ensure that their installations operate at peak efficiency, achieve maximum energy production, and remain reliable assets in the renewable energy landscape.

System Upgrades and Retrofits

Inverter Upgrades

Consider upgrading inverters to more efficient models, especially as technology evolves. Newer inverters often provide higher yields and improved reliability.

Module Replacement

Evaluate the potential benefits of replacing older solar modules with newer, more efficient models, particularly if the existing modules are underperforming or degrading rapidly.

Battery Integration

Explore the integration of energy storage solutions, such as batteries, to capture excess energy for later use and improve grid stability.

Maximizing solar asset efficiency and optimizing site performance are critical objectives for solar operations managers. By implementing proactive monitoring and maintenance practices, conducting energy yield analyses, considering system upgrades, preparing for weather and environmental factors, and exploring energy storage and grid integration solutions, solar operations managers can ensure that their solar assets operate at peak efficiency, resulting in improved energy production, cost savings, and a more sustainable energy future.

[Chapter 6] – Data Security

Data security is crucial for utility solar assets for several reasons:

Asset Protection:

Utility solar assets represent significant investments in infrastructure. Protecting the data associated with these assets helps safeguard the integrity and functionality of the solar facilities. Unauthorized access to critical data could lead to physical damage, operational disruptions, or even theft.

Operational Efficiency:

Solar power facilities rely on data for efficient operation and maintenance. Monitoring energy production, system performance, and potential issues in real-time enables timely intervention and optimization. If this data is compromised, it can lead to operational inefficiencies, decreased performance, and increased downtime.

Financial Implications:

Utility-scale solar projects often involve complex financial models and contracts. Data related to energy production, billing, and financial transactions must be kept secure to prevent fraudulent activities, financial losses, or legal complications. Unauthorized access to financial data could also impact investor confidence and jeopardize the financial viability of the project.

Regulatory Compliance:

The energy sector is subject to various regulations and standards. Compliance with these regulations is essential for legal and ethical operation. Ensuring the security of data helps meet regulatory requirements and avoids penalties or legal consequences that may arise from data breaches.

Grid Stability:

Utility solar assets are integral components of the larger energy grid. Data security is vital to ensure the stable and reliable integration of solar power into the grid. Unauthorized access to control systems or manipulation of data could potentially disrupt grid operations and lead to cascading effects on the entire energy infrastructure.

Privacy Concerns:

Utility solar assets may collect data from various sources, including sensors, weather stations, and customer information for billing purposes. Protecting this data is essential to maintain privacy and comply with privacy laws and regulations, ensuring that sensitive information is not exposed or misused.

Cybersecurity Risks:

As with any digital infrastructure, utility solar assets are susceptible to cybersecurity threats such as hacking, ransomware, or other malicious activities. Ensuring robust cybersecurity measures helps defend against these threats and ensures the continued reliable operation of the solar facilities.

In summary, data security is imperative for utility solar assets to protect investments, maintain operational efficiency, comply with regulations, ensure financial integrity, contribute to grid stability, address privacy concerns, and mitigate cybersecurity risks. It is a fundamental aspect of responsible and sustainable management of utility-scale solar projects.

Data Management and Security

Data Management Systems

Implement robust data management systems that store, organize, and secure the vast amount of data generated by solar installations.

Data Privacy and Security

Adhere to data privacy regulations and ensure data security to protect sensitive information from breaches or cyber threats.

Data Accessibility

Ensure that relevant team members have access to real-time data and analytics tools to facilitate informed decision-making.

Regulatory Compliance

NERC violations in the renewable energy sector, including solar PV facilities, could potentially arise from issues such as improper operation, inadequate maintenance, failure to comply with standards and regulations, lack of proper monitoring and controls, and cybersecurity vulnerabilities.

Common NERC violations for solar PV facilities or any energy facility in the electrical grid could include:

Failure to comply with NERC reliability standards related to solar PV energy integration and grid interconnection.

Inadequate equipment maintenance leading to equipment failures or operational issues.

Violations related to cybersecurity and protecting the solar PV facility from cyber threats.

Failure to properly monitor and control the solar PV facility's operations to ensure grid stability and reliability.

Improper training and qualifications of personnel responsible for operating and maintaining the solar PV facility.

Inadequate reporting or documentation of incidents, maintenance activities, and compliance efforts.

Non-compliance with requirements for monitoring and reporting the solar PV facility's output to the grid operator.

Failure to coordinate with other grid operators or transmission entities for seamless integration and operation of the solar PV facility.

It's essential for solar PV facility operators and owners to stay updated with the latest NERC reliability standards and regulatory requirements to ensure compliance and minimize the risk of violations. NERC regularly updates and revises its standards to enhance grid reliability and security.

Cybersecurity Requirements

To give you an overview of NERC's cybersecurity requirements, they are part of the Critical Infrastructure Protection (CIP) standards. These standards aim to protect the Bulk Electric System (BES) against cybersecurity threats and attacks.

Some of the key CIP standards that address cybersecurity requirements for the electric utility industry include:

CIP-002: Cyber Security – BES Cyber System Categorization: This standard establishes a process for identifying and categorizing BES Cyber Systems based on their criticality to the operation of the Bulk Electric System.

CIP-003: Cyber Security – Security Management Controls: This standard requires entities to implement security management controls to protect BES Cyber Systems from unauthorized access and ensure the security of those systems.

CIP-004: Cyber Security – Personnel and Training: These standard mandates that responsible entities ensure personnel with access to BES Cyber Systems have the necessary training and qualifications to perform their roles securely.

CIP-005: Cyber Security – Electronic Security Perimeter(s): This standard addresses the protection of the Electronic Security Perimeters (ESPs) that provide a boundary between the BES Cyber Systems and external networks.

CIP-007: Cyber Security – System Security Management: This standard requires entities to implement specific security measures for BES Cyber Systems, including incident response and recovery plans.

CIP-010: Cyber Security – Configuration Change Management and Vulnerability Assessments: This standard mandates procedures for managing changes to BES Cyber Systems and conducting regular vulnerability assessments.

CIP-011: Cyber Security – Information Protection: This standard addresses the protection of sensitive information related to the security of the BES Cyber Systems.

CIP-014: Physical Security: This standard focuses on the physical security of critical assets, including facilities and control centers, that are part of the Bulk Electric System.

Please note that these are just some of the key CIP standards related to cybersecurity. NERC's cybersecurity requirements are continuously evolving to address emerging threats and challenges in the energy sector. Utilities and entities subject to NERC's jurisdiction must comply with these standards to ensure the security and reliability of the electric grid.

Security Management Controls

 NERC CIP-003 focuses on security management controls, including the protection of Transient Cyber Assets (TCAs). TCAs are defined as cyber assets that perform a specific task or function with a known start and stop time, such as laptops, mobile devices, and removable media, which are used in conjunction with BES Cyber Systems.

To manage laptops and other transient assets in compliance with CIP-003, you should consider the following practices:

1. Inventory Management: Maintain an up-to-date inventory of all laptops and other transient assets used in conjunction with BES Cyber Systems. This inventory should include the asset's location, owner, purpose, and access controls.

2. Security Awareness Training: Ensure that personnel using transient assets receive appropriate security awareness training. The training should cover safe handling practices, awareness of cybersecurity risks, and adherence to security policies and procedures.

3. Access Control: Implement access controls to restrict unauthorized access to laptops and other transient assets. Only authorized personnel should have access to these assets, and their access should be based on the principle of least privilege.

4. Encryption: Encrypt data stored on laptops and removable media to protect sensitive information in case of loss or theft.

5. Physical Security: Implement physical security measures to prevent unauthorized physical access to laptops and other transient assets. Consider using locks or secure storage when these assets are not in use.

6. Periodic Auditing: Conduct regular audits to verify the accuracy of the inventory and assess the security measures in place for laptops and transient assets.

7. Disposal and Decommissioning: Establish procedures for the secure disposal or decommissioning of laptops and other transient assets when they are no longer needed or have reached the end of their lifecycle.

8. Incident Response: Include laptops and other transient assets in your organization's incident response and recovery plans. In the event of a security incident involving these assets, have procedures in place to address the incident promptly.

9. Remote Access: If laptops or transient assets are used for remote access to BES Cyber Systems, ensure that remote access is secure, and follow best practices for securing remote connections.

It's important to note that cybersecurity standards and requirements can change over time. Therefore, it's crucial to keep abreast of the latest updates and guidance from NERC and the applicable Regional Entities to ensure ongoing compliance with CIP-003 and other relevant standards.

[Chapter 7] - Preparing Site and Team Budgets

Budgeting for Solar Operations

Effective budgeting is a cornerstone of successful solar operations management. Let's explore the strategies and best practices that solar operations managers can employ to create and manage budgets that support the efficient operation of large-scale solar energy projects.

The Importance of Budgeting

Financial Sustainability

Budgeting ensures the financial sustainability of solar operations by allocating resources effectively and planning for both operational and capital expenses.

Resource Allocation

Budgets allocate resources to various aspects of solar operations, such as maintenance, personnel, equipment, and project development, based on priorities and strategic goals.

Risk Mitigation

Budgets serve as a tool for risk mitigation by providing a financial cushion for unforeseen expenses or emergencies.

Performance Monitoring

Budgets provide a framework for performance monitoring, allowing managers to assess whether expenses are in line with projections and make adjustments as needed.

Creating a Solar Operations Budget

Historical Data

Use historical financial data and performance metrics to inform the creation of a new budget. Analyze past expenses, revenues, and operational patterns.

Expense Categories

Identify and categorize the main expense categories, such as personnel costs, maintenance, equipment purchases, utilities, and project development.

Revenue Projections

Estimate revenue sources, including energy sales, incentives, and tax benefits, to determine the total budget size.

Contingency Planning

Incorporate contingency plans into the budget to account for unexpected events or fluctuations in expenses or revenue.

Costs

Staffing Requirements

Determine the staffing requirements for solar operations, considering factors such as site size, complexity, and maintenance needs.

Labor Budget

Allocate a portion of the budget to personnel costs, including salaries, benefits, and training.

Preventive Maintenance

Allocate funds for routine maintenance and preventive measures to ensure equipment reliability and longevity.

This would also include an equipment tooling, and outage preparations based on industry or OEM specifications.

Equipment Procurement

Budget for the purchase and installation of solar modules, inverters, tracking systems, and other equipment, considering both initial costs and ongoing maintenance expenses.

Vegetation Management

Evaluate the budget needed to properly maintain the vegetation on site. This could be a number of different strategies depending on the site. Be sure to take into account safety, wildfire risks, and operational considerations. Some site this could be a significant portion of overall operating costs.

Emergency Repairs

Include provisions for emergency repairs and equipment replacements to minimize downtime and revenue loss.

Utilities

Budget for utility expenses, such as electricity, water, and gas, required for site operation and maintenance.

Insurance

Include insurance costs for property, liability, and equipment coverage to protect against unforeseen events and liabilities.

Outsourcing

Evaluate the cost-effectiveness of outsourcing specific tasks or maintenance activities, and include these expenses in the budget.

Licensing and Compliance

Allocate funds for permits, licenses, and compliance with regulatory requirements.

Project Development and Expansion

New Projects

If planning to expand operations or develop new projects, budget for feasibility studies, land acquisition, permitting, and construction costs.

Return on Investment (ROI) Analysis

Conduct ROI analyses to ensure that new projects align with budgetary constraints and long-term financial goals.

Monitoring and Adjustments

Regular Monitoring

Monitor budget performance regularly to identify discrepancies, overages, or areas where adjustments are needed.

Variance Analysis

Conduct variance analysis to compare budgeted expenses with actual expenses, identifying areas where corrective action is required.

Flexibility

Maintain budget flexibility to adapt to changing circumstances, such as market fluctuations, technological advancements, or regulatory changes.

Reporting and Accountability

Reporting Systems

Implement robust reporting systems that provide stakeholders with clear, accurate, and up-to-date financial information.

Accountability

Hold team members accountable for adhering to budgetary guidelines and provide training as needed to ensure financial responsibility.

Budgeting is a critical component of successful solar operations management. By creating well-informed budgets, monitoring expenses and revenue diligently, and making timely adjustments, solar operations managers can ensure the financial sustainability of their projects, minimize risks, and achieve long-term success in the dynamic renewable energy industry.

Cost Control and Resource Allocation

Cost control and resource allocation are central to efficient and sustainable solar operations management. Let's explore strategies and best practices that solar operations managers can implement to effectively control costs and allocate resources for optimal outcomes.

Cost Control Strategies

Cost-Benefit Analysis

Conduct thorough cost-benefit analyses to evaluate the financial implications of operational decisions and investments in equipment or technology.

Lifecycle Cost Analysis

Consider the entire lifecycle cost of solar assets, including initial installation, maintenance, and decommissioning, to make informed decisions.

Vendor Negotiation

Negotiate with equipment vendors, service providers, and contractors to secure competitive prices and favorable terms.

Energy Efficiency

Implement energy-efficient practices, such as optimizing system parameters and equipment settings, to reduce operational expenses.

Resource Allocation Strategies

Prioritization

Prioritize resource allocation based on criticality and alignment with organizational objectives. Focus on areas that have the most significant impact on performance and profitability.

Risk Assessment

Conduct risk assessments to identify potential resource allocation challenges and develop strategies to mitigate them.

Cross-Training

Cross-train team members to enhance resource flexibility and ensure that key roles can be filled during staff shortages or emergencies.

Technology Investments

Allocate resources to technology investments, such as monitoring systems and data analytics tools, that enhance operational efficiency and decision-making.

Resource Optimization

Personnel Utilization

Optimize personnel deployment to ensure that staff members are assigned tasks that align with their skills and expertise.

Preventive Maintenance

Allocate resources to preventive maintenance activities, which can reduce the need for costly emergency repairs.

Asset Utilization

Maximize the utilization of solar assets by implementing tracking systems and optimizing module angles for maximum sun exposure.

Energy Storage

Allocate resources to energy storage solutions that capture excess energy for use during peak demand, potentially reducing operational expenses.

Monitoring and Control Mechanisms

Key Performance Indicators (KPIs)

Establish KPIs for cost control and resource allocation, regularly monitor them, and use them to make data-driven decisions.

Budget Adherence

Implement budgetary controls and regularly review expenses to ensure adherence to budgetary guidelines.

Continuous Improvement

Foster a culture of continuous improvement, where team members are encouraged to identify cost-saving opportunities and operational enhancements.

Sustainable Practices

Environmental Considerations

Consider sustainability and environmental practices when allocating resources, including choices related to equipment, materials, and waste management.

Sustainable Procurement

Seek out suppliers and vendors who prioritize sustainability and align with your organization's environmental goals.

Flexibility and Adaptability

Contingency Planning

Incorporate contingency plans into resource allocation strategies to address unexpected events, such as equipment failures or adverse weather conditions.

Scalability

Design resource allocation plans with scalability in mind to accommodate changes in the scale of solar operations.

Regulatory Compliance

Allocate resources for regulatory compliance to avoid penalties and legal challenges that could impact project finances.

Cost control and resource allocation are vital aspects of efficient solar operations management. By implementing cost-effective strategies, optimizing resource allocation, monitoring performance, and fostering a culture of continuous improvement, solar operations managers can ensure the financial sustainability and long-term success of their solar energy projects.

Long-Term Financial Planning

Long-term financial planning is a strategic endeavor that sets the course for the financial sustainability and growth of solar energy projects. Let's dig into the strategies and best practices that solar operations managers can employ to develop and execute effective long-term financial plans.

The Importance of Long-Term Financial Planning

Financial Sustainability

Long-term financial planning ensures the sustainability of solar energy projects by addressing future financial needs and challenges.

Strategic Decision-Making

It supports strategic decision-making by providing a roadmap for resource allocation, investments, and risk management over an extended period.

Risk Mitigation

Long-term financial planning identifies and mitigates potential financial risks, fostering stability and resilience in the face of uncertainty.

Components of Long-Term Financial Planning

Financial Forecasting

Utilize historical financial data and market trends to create forecasts that project income, expenses, and cash flow over an extended timeframe.

Scenario Analysis

Conduct scenario analysis to explore various financial scenarios and assess their impact on long-term sustainability.

Investment Planning

Identify opportunities for capital investments, technology upgrades, and expansion, aligning them with long-term financial goals.

Debt Management

Develop strategies for managing debt, including refinancing options, repayment schedules, and interest rate risk mitigation.

Risk Management

Risk Assessment

Conduct comprehensive risk assessments to identify financial, operational, and market risks that could impact the project's long-term financial health.

Risk Mitigation Strategies

Develop risk mitigation strategies that include insurance coverage, hedging against market volatility, and financial reserves for unforeseen challenges.

Regulatory Compliance

Stay informed about changing regulatory requirements and allocate resources to ensure ongoing compliance.

Asset Management and Performance Optimization

Asset Lifecycle Planning

Develop plans for managing assets throughout their lifecycle, including maintenance, upgrades, and end-of-life considerations.

Performance Optimization

Implement strategies for optimizing asset performance and energy production over the long term, which can have a significant impact on financial returns.

Reporting and Accountability

Reporting Systems

Establish robust reporting systems that provide stakeholders with transparent and accurate financial information regarding long-term planning and performance.

Accountability

Hold team members accountable for adhering to long-term financial plans and regularly review progress toward established goals.

Flexibility and Adaptability

Periodic Review

Periodically review and adjust long-term financial plans to accommodate changing circumstances, such as market conditions, technological advancements, and regulatory changes.

Contingency Planning

Incorporate contingency plans into long-term financial planning to address unforeseen events that could impact financial stability.

Scalability

Design long-term financial plans with scalability in mind, allowing for the expansion or contraction of solar operations as needed.

Sustainability and Environmental Considerations

Sustainability Goals

Integrate sustainability goals into long-term financial planning, considering practices that minimize environmental impact and align with ESG (Environmental, Social, and Governance) principles.

Environmental Compliance

Allocate resources for environmental compliance, ensuring that projects meet or exceed regulatory requirements.

Long-term financial planning is a critical aspect of effective solar operations management. By developing comprehensive financial forecasts, assessing risks, aligning investments with long-term goals, and maintaining flexibility and adaptability, solar operations managers can ensure the financial sustainability and growth of their solar energy projects over the years.

[Chapter 8] - Handling Major Equipment Failures

Identifying Common Equipment Failures

Failure management is a crucial aspect of solar operations management, as equipment failures can have a significant impact on energy production and project profitability. Let's explore strategies for managing failures and identifying common equipment failures in solar installations.

The Impact of Equipment Failures

Reduced Energy Production

Equipment failures can lead to reduced energy production, resulting in revenue losses and potential contractual penalties.

Increased Maintenance Costs

Failures often necessitate emergency repairs and maintenance, which can be costly and disrupt daily operations.

Safety Concerns

Certain equipment failures pose safety risks to personnel and the environment, underscoring the importance of swift response and mitigation.

Reputation Concerns

Maintaining assets with high availability creates a trust and assurance for investors, owners, and communities. When assets underperform or have significant issues this can impact reputation of the service provider and /or industry.

Identifying Common Equipment Failures

Inverter Failures

Inverters are critical components that convert DC power generated by solar modules into AC power for the grid. Common failures include voltage fluctuations, overheating, and component degradation.

Solar Module Failures

Solar modules may experience reduced efficiency due to factors like soiling, shading, or cell degradation. Physical damage, such as cracks or hotspots, can also occur.

Tracking System Failures

Tracking systems, if present, can experience motor malfunctions, misalignment, or sensor errors, leading to suboptimal sun exposure.

Cabling and Electrical Failures

Issues with electrical connections, wiring, or junction boxes can result in electrical faults or even fires if not addressed promptly.

Sensor and Monitoring System Failures

Failures in sensors or monitoring systems can lead to data inaccuracies and hinder the ability to detect and respond to performance deviations.

Failure Management Strategies

Maintenance

Conduct routine inspections of all equipment to identify early signs of wear, damage, or performance anomalies.

Leverage predictive maintenance techniques, such as thermographic imaging and vibration analysis, to detect equipment issues before they lead to failure.

Spare Parts Inventory

Maintain an inventory of critical spare parts, allowing for quick replacements and minimizing downtime.

Vendor Relationships

Foster strong relationships with equipment vendors and service providers to ensure timely support during equipment failures and repairs.

Emergency Response Plans

Develop and maintain emergency response plans that outline procedures for addressing equipment failures, including resource allocation and communication protocols.

Data Analytics for Failure Prediction

Data-Driven Insights

Utilize data analytics and machine learning to analyze historical performance data and identify patterns or anomalies that could indicate impending failures.

Anomaly Detection

Implement anomaly detection algorithms that automatically flag irregularities in equipment performance or sensor data.

Condition Monitoring

Deploy condition monitoring systems that continuously assess the health of critical equipment, providing early warnings of potential failures.

Safety and Environmental Considerations

Safety Protocols

Develop and communicate safety protocols for responding to equipment failures, emphasizing the importance of safety in all failure management efforts.

Environmental Compliance

Ensure that failure response activities comply with environmental regulations, including waste disposal and hazardous material handling.

Documentation and Post-Failure Analysis

Incident Reporting

Implement incident reporting systems to document equipment failures, responses, and resolutions.

Root Cause Analysis

Conduct thorough root cause analyses to understand the underlying reasons for failures and implement preventive measures to avoid recurrence.

Performance Evaluation

Evaluate the performance of the failure response process and adjust procedures as needed for continuous improvement.

Identifying and managing equipment failures is a critical aspect of solar operations management. By implementing proactive inspection and maintenance practices, leveraging data analytics for failure prediction, and establishing robust emergency response plans, solar operations managers can minimize the impact of failures on energy production and project profitability.

Crisis Management and Contingency Planning

Crisis management and contingency planning are essential aspects of solar operations management, ensuring that solar energy projects can withstand unforeseen challenges and disruptions. Let's explore strategies and best practices for effectively managing crises and developing robust contingency plans.

The Significance of Crisis Management

Unpredictable Events

Crisis management is vital because unexpected events, such as extreme weather, equipment failures, or regulatory changes, can threaten the operation and financial viability of solar projects.

Minimizing Impact

Effective crisis management aims to minimize the impact of crises on energy production, safety, and financial stability.

Reputation Management

Well-handled crises can positively impact the reputation of solar projects and organizations by demonstrating resilience and responsible management.

Developing a Contingency Plan

Risk Assessment

Conduct a thorough risk assessment to identify potential crises and their impact on solar operations.

Response Teams

Establish dedicated response teams with clearly defined roles and responsibilities for managing different types of crises.

Communication Protocols

Define communication protocols for internal and external stakeholders, ensuring that accurate information is disseminated promptly during a crisis.

Resource Allocation

Determine resource allocation strategies, including access to financial reserves and emergency equipment.

Scenario Planning

Develop contingency plans for various crisis scenarios, outlining specific actions, timelines, and resource requirements.

Types of Solar Crisis

Natural Disasters

Prepare for natural disasters, such as hurricanes, wildfires, or floods, by implementing evacuation plans, securing equipment, and having backup power sources in place.

Equipment Failures

Create response plans for equipment failures, including spare parts inventory and relationships with service providers for rapid repairs.

Regulatory Changes

Stay informed about regulatory changes that could impact solar projects, and have legal and compliance strategies in place.

Financial Crises

Plan for financial crises by maintaining financial reserves and exploring financing options to cover unexpected expenses.

Cybersecurity Incidents

Develop cybersecurity measures to protect solar assets from potential cyberattacks or data breaches.

Crisis Response Protocols

Immediate Response

Outline immediate response protocols for rapid action during the early stages of a crisis, including safety procedures and emergency notifications.

Stakeholder Communication

Establish clear communication channels and messaging for stakeholders, including employees, investors, customers, and the public.

Resource Deployment

Coordinate the deployment of resources, such as personnel, equipment, and financial reserves, to address the crisis effectively.

Containment and Mitigation

Implement strategies for containing the crisis and mitigating its impact on energy production and safety.

Recovery and Restoration

Develop plans for the recovery and restoration of solar operations once the crisis has been managed.

Post-Crisis Evaluation and Improvement

After-Action Review

Conduct after-action reviews to assess the effectiveness of the crisis response and identify areas for improvement.

Continuous Training

Continuously train response teams and update contingency plans to adapt to evolving risks and challenges.

Stakeholder Feedback

Seek feedback from stakeholders on the crisis response to refine future strategies.

Crisis management and contingency planning are essential for safeguarding solar energy projects against unforeseen challenges. By proactively identifying potential crises, developing comprehensive contingency plans, and executing crisis response protocols effectively, solar operations managers can protect the stability, reputation, and long-term success of their projects.

[Chapter 9] - Communicating with Senior Leadership

Presenting Key Metrics and Performance Data

Effective communication with leadership is pivotal in solar operations management, as it ensures that key decision-makers are well-informed about the performance, challenges, and opportunities of solar projects. Let's explore strategies and best practices for communicating with leadership and presenting key metrics and performance data.

The Importance of Communication with Leadership

Informed Decision-Making

Effective communication with leadership ensures that decision-makers have the necessary information to make informed choices that impact the success of solar projects.

Alignment with Goals

It aligns the operational efforts with the organization's strategic goals and financial objectives.

Risk Management

Regular communication allows leadership to stay informed about potential risks and challenges, facilitating proactive risk management.

Accountability

Communication holds teams accountable for their performance and encourages a culture of transparency and responsibility.

Key Metrics and Performance Data

Energy Production

Present data on energy production, including daily, monthly, and yearly figures, to showcase the project's performance in generating renewable energy.

Revenue and Expenses

Provide financial data, including revenue, expenses, and profitability metrics, to illustrate the project's financial health.

Equipment Performance

Detail equipment performance data, such as inverter efficiency, solar module degradation rates, and uptime statistics.

Maintenance and Repairs

Report on maintenance activities, including preventive measures, equipment repairs, and their impact on operational downtime.

Effective Communication Strategies

Audience Understanding

Tailor communication to the specific needs and understanding of the leadership audience, avoiding technical jargon when necessary.

Clear Visualization

Utilize clear and visually engaging presentations, charts, graphs, and dashboards to convey complex data effectively.

Regular Updates

Provide regular updates, whether weekly, monthly, or quarterly, to keep leadership informed about ongoing progress and developments.

Highlighting Challenges

Be transparent about challenges and setbacks and discuss strategies for addressing them.

Solutions and Opportunities

Present solutions and opportunities for improvement, demonstrating a proactive approach to addressing issues.

Reporting on Sustainability and ESG Metrics

Sustainability Metrics

Include sustainability metrics related to environmental impact, such as carbon emissions reduction, water usage, and waste management.

ESG (Environmental, Social, and Governance) Reporting

Discuss the organization's commitment to ESG principles, including social responsibility and ethical governance.

Compliance

Report on compliance with environmental regulations and any initiatives related to renewable energy credits or incentives.

Risk and Contingency Reporting

Risk Assessment

Provide updates on risk assessments and mitigation strategies, keeping leadership informed about potential threats to the project.

Contingency Plans

Discuss contingency plans and crisis management protocols, reassuring leadership that the project is prepared to handle unexpected challenges.

Financial Health

Highlight the financial health of the project, emphasizing the availability of financial reserves for emergencies.

Interactive Engagement

Q&A Sessions

Encourage open dialogue by including question-and-answer sessions in presentations, allowing leadership to seek clarification and provide input.

Feedback Channels

Establish feedback channels where leadership can provide insights, concerns, and suggestions related to solar operations.

Site Visits

Arrange site visits to provide leadership with a firsthand look at solar installations and their performance.

Effective communication with leadership and the presentation of key metrics and performance data are essential elements of successful solar operations management. By conveying information clearly, tailoring communication to the audience, and fostering an environment of transparency and collaboration, solar operations managers can ensure that leadership remains well-informed and engaged in decision-making processes.

Making the Business Case for Solar Investments

In the dynamic landscape of renewable energy, making a compelling business case for solar investments is crucial to securing financial support and ensuring the success of solar projects. Let's explore strategies and best practices for effectively presenting the business case for solar investments to stakeholders, including investors, financiers, and decision-makers.

The Importance of a Strong Business Case

Securing Financial Support

A strong business case is essential for attracting investors, securing financing, and obtaining approvals for solar projects.

Risk Mitigation

A well-documented business case demonstrates a clear understanding of potential risks and outlines strategies for risk mitigation.

Aligning with Strategic Goals

The business case should align with the organization's strategic goals, emphasizing the contribution of solar investments to overall objectives.

Stakeholder Engagement

It serves as a tool for engaging stakeholders by providing a transparent and compelling rationale for solar investments.

Components of the Business Case

Market Analysis

Conduct a thorough market analysis to identify opportunities, demand for renewable energy, and competitive positioning.

Technical Feasibility

Present a technical feasibility assessment that outlines the solar project's design, technology, and expected energy production.

Financial Projections

Include detailed financial projections, covering capital costs, operational expenses, revenue forecasts, and return on investment (ROI) calculations.

Risk Assessment

Identify and assess potential risks, such as regulatory changes, equipment failures, and market volatility, and outline strategies for risk mitigation.

Environmental and Social Impact

Highlight the positive environmental and social impact of solar investments, emphasizing sustainability and corporate responsibility.

Building a Compelling Narrative

Clarity and Simplicity

Present information in a clear and straightforward manner, avoiding unnecessary jargon or complexity.

Storytelling

Craft a narrative that resonates with stakeholders, showcasing the project's mission, vision, and potential benefits.

Visual Aids

Incorporate visual aids, such as charts, graphs, and infographics, to enhance understanding and engagement.

Real-World Examples

Provide real-world examples and case studies to illustrate the success of similar solar investments.

Financial Analysis and ROI

Investment Analysis

Conduct a thorough investment analysis, including net present value (NPV), internal rate of return (IRR), and payback period calculations.

Sensitivity Analysis

Perform sensitivity analysis to assess the impact of variables like changes in energy prices or equipment costs on the project's financial viability.

Risk-Adjusted Returns

Consider risk-adjusted returns, factoring in potential risks and uncertainties when presenting ROI figures.

Regulatory and Incentive Considerations

Regulatory Compliance

Demonstrate awareness of and compliance with local, state, and federal regulations governing solar investments.

Incentives and Tax Benefits

Highlight available incentives, tax benefits, and renewable energy credits that enhance the financial attractiveness of the project.

Regulatory Advocacy

Advocate for favorable regulatory policies that support solar investments, when applicable.

Stakeholder Engagement

Investor Relations

Engage potential investors and financiers early in the process, keeping them informed and involved in project developments.

Decision-Maker Briefings

Provide decision-makers with comprehensive briefings that address their specific concerns and priorities.

Community Outreach

Engage with local communities and stakeholders to build support and address concerns related to solar projects.

Continuous Improvement

Post-Implementation Evaluation

After project implementation, evaluate the actual performance and financial outcomes compared to the business case projections.

Lessons Learned

Identify lessons learned and areas for improvement to enhance the accuracy and effectiveness of future business cases.

Making a persuasive business case for solar investments is a critical step in securing the necessary support and resources for solar projects.

Aligning Solar Operations with Organizational Goals

Alignment between solar operations and organizational goals is essential for ensuring that solar energy projects contribute effectively to an organization's broader mission, objectives, and sustainability commitments. Let's explore strategies and best practices for aligning solar operations with organizational goals.

The Importance of Alignment

Strategic Integration

Aligning solar operations with organizational goals ensures that renewable energy initiatives are strategically integrated into the overall business strategy.

Sustainability Commitments

Organizations committed to sustainability and corporate responsibility can use solar operations to demonstrate their dedication to reducing their environmental footprint.

Financial Objectives

Alignment supports financial objectives by enhancing cost savings, improving energy efficiency, and contributing to revenue generation.

Stakeholder Expectations

Meeting the expectations of stakeholders, including investors, customers, and regulators, is facilitated through alignment with sustainability and environmental goals.

Defining Organizational Goals

Mission and Vision

Start by understanding the organization's mission and vision, which provide a high-level framework for aligning solar operations.

Sustainability Targets

Identify specific sustainability targets and environmental objectives that solar operations can help achieve.

Financial Objectives

Consider financial objectives, such as reducing energy costs or generating revenue through energy sales, that align with solar operations.

Regulatory Compliance

Ensure compliance with regulatory requirements and environmental standards that affect the organization's operations.

Strategies for Alignment

Cross-Functional Collaboration

Facilitate collaboration between solar operations teams and other departments to ensure alignment with broader organizational goals.

Goal Cascading

Cascade organizational goals down to specific solar projects, ensuring that each project contributes to the achievement of higher-level objectives.

Performance Metrics

Develop key performance indicators (KPIs) that reflect progress toward organizational goals and regularly track and report on these metrics.

Resource Allocation

Allocate resources, both financial and human, in a manner that prioritizes projects and initiatives aligned with organizational goals.

Communicating Alignment

Internal Communication

Effectively communicate alignment with organizational goals to internal stakeholders, including employees and management.

External Communication

Demonstrate alignment with external stakeholders, such as customers, investors, and regulatory bodies, through transparent reporting and public disclosures.

Stakeholder Engagement

Engage with stakeholders to gather feedback and insights on how solar operations can further align with their expectations.

Continuous Improvement

Regular Evaluation

Continuously evaluate the alignment of solar operations with organizational goals and make adjustments as needed.

Benchmarking

Benchmark against industry standards and best practices to identify opportunities for improvement and innovation.

Innovation

Encourage innovation within solar operations to discover new ways to align with evolving organizational goals.

Aligning solar operations with organizational goals is fundamental to achieving success in renewable energy projects. By defining clear goals, fostering cross-functional collaboration, and communicating alignment effectively, solar operations managers can ensure that their projects contribute meaningfully to the organization's mission, sustainability commitments, and financial objectives.

[Chapter 10] - Sustainability and Environmental Compliance

Navigating Regulatory Requirements

Navigating regulatory requirements is a critical aspect of successful solar operations management. Understanding and complying with local, state, federal, and international regulations is essential to ensure the legal and efficient operation of solar energy projects.

The Regulatory Landscape

Diverse Regulations

Recognize that the regulatory landscape for solar energy can vary widely by location and may encompass zoning laws, permitting requirements, environmental regulations, tax incentives, and more.

Evolving Regulations

Stay informed about changing regulations, as the solar energy industry is subject to ongoing policy developments and revisions.

International Considerations

For global solar projects, be aware of international agreements and standards that may impact operations, such as trade agreements and emissions reduction commitments.

Regulatory Compliance Strategies

Regulatory Team

Establish a dedicated regulatory team or designate individuals within the organization to monitor, interpret, and implement regulations.

Legal Counsel

Engage legal counsel with expertise in energy and environmental law to provide guidance on regulatory matters.

Regular Updates

Maintain a regulatory compliance calendar that tracks deadlines for permits, reports, and other compliance-related activities.

Risk Assessment

Conduct periodic risk assessments to identify potential regulatory risks and liabilities.

Permitting and Approvals

Permit Applications

Ensure that all required permits are submitted accurately and on time, including environmental impact assessments and land-use permits.

Local Engagement

Engage with local authorities, communities, and residents to address concerns and gain support for permit approvals.

Compliance Audits

Regularly audit compliance with permits and approvals to ensure ongoing adherence to regulations.

Environmental Regulations

Environmental Impact

Understand the environmental regulations that apply to solar projects, including habitat protection, water usage, and waste management.

Emissions Reporting

Comply with emissions reporting requirements, which may include greenhouse gas emissions, air quality standards, and hazardous materials management.

Wildlife Protection

Implement wildlife protection measures, such as bird-friendly designs for solar installations.

Export and Trade Regulations

Trade Agreements

Navigate export and trade regulations, especially when dealing with international solar projects subject to trade agreements.

Import Tariffs

Monitor and address import tariffs and trade restrictions that could impact the cost of solar equipment.

Reporting and Documentation

Comprehensive Records

Maintain thorough records of regulatory compliance activities, including permits, reports, inspections, and correspondence.

Reporting Deadlines

Meet reporting deadlines for emissions, safety, and environmental compliance to avoid penalties.

Audits and Inspections

Prepare for audits and inspections by regulatory authorities by ensuring that all necessary documentation is readily available.

Navigating regulatory requirements in solar operations is a complex but necessary endeavor. By establishing a strong regulatory compliance strategy, engaging with legal counsel, staying informed about evolving regulations, and maintaining meticulous records, solar operations managers can ensure that their projects not only comply with the law but also operate efficiently and sustainably within the regulatory framework.

Implementing Sustainable Practices

Implementing sustainable practices in solar operations is essential not only for reducing environmental impact but also for enhancing the long-term viability and success of solar energy projects. Let's explore strategies and best practices for integrating sustainability into solar operations.

The Significance of Sustainability

Environmental Responsibility

Sustainability in solar operations reflects a commitment to environmental responsibility by reducing carbon emissions and minimizing resource consumption.

Cost Savings

Sustainable practices often lead to cost savings through energy efficiency, reduced waste, and lower operational expenses.

Stakeholder Expectations

Meeting the sustainability expectations of investors, customers, and communities is essential for maintaining a positive reputation.

Regulatory Compliance

Many regulatory requirements mandate sustainability practices, making compliance crucial for solar operations.

Environmental Impact Reduction

Habitat Protection

Implement habitat protection measures, such as wildlife-friendly designs and land management practices that minimize ecological disruption.

Water Conservation

Minimize water usage through efficient cooling systems and consider rainwater harvesting for irrigation and other non-potable needs.

Waste Management

> Develop effective waste management strategies, including recycling and responsible disposal of hazardous materials.

Sustainable Supply Chain

Ethical Sourcing

> Source solar equipment and materials from suppliers committed to ethical and sustainable practices.

Life Cycle Assessment

> Conduct life cycle assessments of solar equipment to understand the environmental impact throughout their entire life span.

Supplier Engagement

> Engage with suppliers to encourage sustainability initiatives and collaboration in reducing the environmental footprint of solar installations.

Implementing sustainable practices in solar operations is integral to achieving long-term success and environmental responsibility. By focusing on sustainable energy production, reducing environmental impact, engaging with stakeholders, and transparently reporting on sustainability efforts, solar operations managers can lead their projects toward a more sustainable and resilient future.

Reporting and Certification

Reporting and certification play a vital role in demonstrating the performance, sustainability, and compliance of solar energy projects. Let's explore the significance of reporting and certification in solar operations and discuss best practices for effectively managing these aspects.

The Importance of Reporting and Certification

Transparency

Reporting and certification enhance transparency by providing stakeholders with accurate and verifiable information about solar operations.

Accountability

Certifications and reporting mechanisms hold solar projects accountable for their environmental, social, and financial commitments.

Credibility

Certifications from reputable organizations enhance the credibility of solar projects, making them more attractive to investors and customers.

Regulatory Compliance

Reporting ensures compliance with local, state, federal, and international regulations, reducing the risk of legal issues.

Types of Reporting and Certification

Environmental Reporting

This includes reporting on carbon emissions, water usage, waste management, and other environmental impact factors.

Financial Reporting

Financial reports provide information on revenue, expenses, profitability, and return on investment (ROI).

Sustainability Certifications

Obtaining certifications such as LEED (Leadership in Energy and Environmental Design) or ISO 14001 demonstrates commitment to sustainability.

Health and Safety Certification

Certifications like OHSAS 18001 or ISO 45001 showcase adherence to health and safety standards.

Quality Certification

Quality certifications like ISO 9001 highlight the commitment to quality management systems.

Effective Reporting Strategies

Clear Documentation

Maintain clear and comprehensive documentation of all relevant data, including energy production, equipment maintenance, and financial transactions.

Regular Updates

Provide regular updates and reports to stakeholders, adhering to predefined reporting schedules.

Key Performance Indicators (KPIs)

Define and track KPIs that are relevant to your solar operations, such as energy output, downtime, or emissions reductions.

Data Visualization

Present data in visually engaging formats, such as charts, graphs, and dashboards, to improve understanding.

Sustainability Certifications

ISO 14001 Certification

ISO 14001 certification demonstrates commitment to environmental management systems and sustainability practices.

B Corp Certification

B Corp certification reflects a commitment to social and environmental performance, transparency, and accountability.

Third-Party Verification

Independent Audits

Engage third-party auditors to independently verify and validate your reporting and certifications.

Credibility Assurance

Third-party verification enhances the credibility of your reporting and certifications in the eyes of stakeholders.

Continuous Improvement

Use the feedback and insights from third-party audits to continuously improve your operations and reporting processes.

Transparency and Stakeholder Engagement

Communication

Effectively communicate your reporting and certification results to stakeholders, including investors, customers, and the public.

Stakeholder Input

Engage with stakeholders to gather feedback and insights on your reporting and sustainability efforts.

Addressing Concerns

Address any concerns or questions raised by stakeholders related to your reporting and certification practices.

By adopting effective reporting strategies, pursuing relevant certifications, ensuring regulatory compliance, and engaging with stakeholders, solar operations managers can demonstrate their commitment to responsible and sustainable solar energy initiatives.

[Chapter 11] - Future Trends and Innovations

Emerging Technologies in Solar Operations

The field of solar operations is continuously evolving with the introduction of new technologies that improve efficiency, reduce costs, and enhance sustainability. Let's explore the most promising emerging technologies in solar operations and their potential impact on the industry.

The Dynamics of Emerging Technologies

Continuous Advancements

Solar operations benefit from ongoing technological advancements, driving innovation in the industry.

Enhanced Performance

Emerging technologies have the potential to significantly enhance the performance and profitability of solar energy projects.

Sustainability and Efficiency

Many emerging technologies focus on increasing sustainability and energy efficiency, aligning with global sustainability goals.

Advanced Monitoring and Control Systems

Artificial Intelligence (AI) and Machine Learning

AI algorithms can predict energy generation, optimize operations, and detect equipment faults more effectively.

Remote Monitoring and IoT

IoT devices and remote monitoring technologies enable real-time data collection and analysis for improved decision-making.

Blockchain for Energy Trading

Blockchain technology can facilitate peer-to-peer energy trading, allowing solar operators to sell excess energy directly to consumers.

Robotics and Drones

Solar Module Cleaning Robots

Automated cleaning robots ensure modules remain free of dust and dirt, maintaining optimal energy production.

Inspections

Drones or robotics equipped with cameras and sensors can perform inspections, identifying maintenance needs and potential issues.

Grid Integration and Microgrids

Grid-Forming Inverters

Grid-forming inverters enhance the stability and resilience of solar installations, enabling seamless grid integration.

Microgrids

Microgrids allow solar operations to operate independently or interact with the larger grid as needed, increasing reliability.

Virtual Power Plants

Virtual power plants aggregate the energy generation and storage capabilities of distributed solar installations, providing grid support.

Emerging technologies are shaping the future of solar operations, offering opportunities for improved performance, efficiency, and sustainability. Solar operations managers should remain vigilant in monitoring these advancements and assess their applicability to their projects to stay competitive and environmentally responsible.

Integrating Energy Storage and Grid Connectivity

Integrating energy storage and grid connectivity is a transformative step in enhancing the reliability, flexibility, and efficiency of solar energy operations. Let's explore the significance of energy storage and grid connectivity, as well as best practices for their seamless integration into solar operations.

The Importance of Integration

Enhanced Reliability

Energy storage improves reliability by providing a stable source of power, reducing the impact of intermittent solar energy generation.

Grid Support

Integrated systems can provide grid support, including voltage regulation and peak demand shaving, benefiting both solar operators and the grid.

Energy Resilience

Energy storage enhances energy resilience by providing backup power during grid outages or emergencies.

Increased Self-Consumption

Integrated systems enable solar operators to consume more of the energy they generate, reducing reliance on the grid.

Energy Storage Technologies

Battery Energy Storage

Battery technologies, such as lithium-ion, lead-acid, and emerging chemistries, offer scalable and efficient energy storage solutions.

Thermal Energy Storage

Thermal storage systems use heat or cold storage to manage energy for later use, complementing solar heating and cooling applications.

Grid Connectivity Solutions

Grid-Tied Systems

Grid-tied solar operations remain connected to the grid, allowing for energy export, grid support, and access to backup power.

Microgrids

Microgrids can operate independently or in coordination with the grid, ensuring reliable energy supply and grid support during outages.

Virtual Power Plants (VPPs)

VPPs aggregate distributed energy resources, including solar and storage, to provide grid services and enhance energy market participation.

Grid-Forming Inverters

Grid-forming inverters help stabilize microgrids and enhance grid integration, enabling seamless transition between grid-connected and islanded modes.

Benefits and Challenges

Benefits of Integration

- Increased energy self-sufficiency.

- Improved response to grid demand fluctuations.

- Enhanced utilization of excess solar energy.

- Grid support services, such as frequency regulation and voltage control.

Challenges of Integration

- High initial investment costs.

- Complex system design and integration.

- Regulatory and policy considerations.

- Battery degradation and maintenance.

The integration of energy storage and grid connectivity is pivotal in maximizing the potential of solar energy projects. By carefully selecting appropriate energy storage technologies, embracing grid connectivity solutions, and addressing challenges through best practices, solar operations managers can create resilient, efficient, and sustainable energy systems that benefit both their operations and the broader grid infrastructure.

Adapting to Changing Market Dynamics

The solar energy market is characterized by dynamic shifts in technology, policy, and market conditions. To thrive in this ever-evolving landscape, solar operations managers must adapt and respond effectively to these changes. Let's explore the importance of adapting to changing market dynamics and strategies for doing so.

The Dynamic Solar Market

Technological Advancements

Rapid advancements in solar technology, such as new module designs and energy storage solutions, continually reshape the market.

Policy and Regulatory Changes

Government policies, incentives, and regulations significantly influence the solar market, with updates and revisions occurring regularly.

Market Competition

Increased competition among solar operators, suppliers, and installers can impact market dynamics and pricing structures.

Economic Factors

Economic conditions, including energy prices and investor sentiment, have a direct bearing on solar project viability.

The Imperative of Adaptation

Staying Competitive

Adaptation is essential for remaining competitive in the solar market and capitalizing on emerging opportunities.

Sustainability Goals

Aligning with changing market dynamics enables solar operations to contribute more effectively to sustainability goals.

Innovation and Growth

Adaptation fosters innovation and growth by encouraging the exploration of new technologies and business models.

Technology Assessment

Regularly assess the feasibility of adopting emerging technologies, such as advanced modules or energy storage solutions.

Scalability

Implement technologies and systems that can be scaled to meet changing energy demands or project sizes.

Financial Modelling

Regularly update financial models to assess the impact of changing economic conditions on project economics.

Risk Management

Implement risk management strategies, such as hedging energy prices or diversifying revenue streams, to mitigate economic volatility.

Strategic Planning

Engage in strategic planning exercises to anticipate and respond to economic shifts effectively.

Adapting to changing market dynamics is a fundamental aspect of successful solar operations management. By proactively monitoring and responding to technological advancements, policy changes, economic conditions, and competitive pressures, solar operations managers can position their projects to thrive in a dynamic and evolving solar energy market.

Lessons Learned and Best Practices

1. Continuous Monitoring and Maintenance: Regular and thorough monitoring and maintenance are essential to ensuring optimal performance. Solar managers should implement a proactive maintenance schedule that includes cleaning modules, checking for wear and tear, and addressing any issues promptly.

2. Weather Variability: Solar energy generation is subject to weather variability. Solar managers should factor in weather patterns and seasonal changes when estimating energy production and revenue. Diversifying energy sources or incorporating energy storage can mitigate the impact of weather fluctuations.

3. Degradation Over Time: Solar modules degrade over time, leading to reduced efficiency. Managers should incorporate degradation rates into their financial models and consider module replacement or refurbishment strategies as modules age.

4. Energy Storage Challenges: While energy storage enhances flexibility and grid support, it also presents challenges such as battery degradation and maintenance. Solar managers should carefully assess the cost-benefit of energy storage solutions and consider factors like the lifetime of batteries and their impact on project economics.

5. Regulatory Changes: Solar operations are highly influenced by government policies and regulations. Managers must stay informed about changes in regulations and incentives, which can significantly impact project viability. Advocacy efforts can also be employed to shape favorable policies.

6. Grid Connectivity: Grid integration is crucial, but it can also pose challenges such as grid congestion or voltage regulation issues. Managers should work closely with grid operators to ensure seamless integration and explore grid-forming inverter technologies to enhance grid support.

7. Economic Considerations: Economic factors, including energy prices and interest rates, can affect project profitability. Solar managers should regularly update financial models, conduct sensitivity analyses, and employ risk mitigation strategies like hedging to manage economic uncertainties.

8. Environmental Responsibility: Environmental practices are vital for long-term success. Solar managers should invest in wildlife protection measures, habitat restoration, and sustainable land use to minimize environmental impact and foster goodwill in local communities.

9. Community Engagement: Building positive relationships with local communities is essential. Managers should engage with stakeholders, address concerns, and consider community solar projects to involve residents directly in solar initiatives.

10. Emerging Technologies: Keeping abreast of emerging technologies is critical. Solar managers should evaluate the feasibility of adopting new technologies such as advanced modules, energy storage, or AI-based predictive maintenance to improve project efficiency and competitiveness.

11. Flexibility in Project Design: Project design should allow for flexibility to accommodate technology upgrades or changes in energy needs. Scalability and adaptability are key considerations during project planning.

12. Compliance and Reporting: Stringent compliance with regulatory requirements and transparent reporting are essential for maintaining credibility and securing long-term investments. Developing robust systems for regulatory compliance is imperative.

13. Diversification: Diversifying solar project portfolios across different geographies or market segments can reduce risks associated with market volatility and regional factors.

14. Investor Relations: Building and maintaining strong relationships with investors and financial stakeholders is crucial for securing funding and support for solar projects.

15. Training and Education: Ongoing training and education for personnel ensure that the team is equipped to handle new technologies, regulatory changes, and evolving best practices.

Incorporating these lessons learned into solar asset management strategies can help solar managers navigate the complex and ever-evolving landscape of the solar energy industry, ultimately leading to more successful and sustainable solar operations.

Conclusion

The Evolving Role of Solar Operations Managers

The role of solar operations managers has evolved significantly over the years, driven by advancements in technology, changes in the energy landscape, and increasing emphasis on sustainability. Let's explore how the role of solar operations managers has transformed and the key responsibilities and skills required in this evolving field.

Historical Perspective

Early Days of Solar Operations

Solar operations management initially focused on basic system maintenance and ensuring energy production.

Expansion of Solar Energy

As solar energy gained prominence, operations managers faced the challenge of managing larger and more complex installations.

Transition to Sustainable Energy

The shift toward sustainable energy solutions brought greater attention to the environmental impact of solar operations.

Modern Role of Solar Operations Managers

Technology Integration

Solar operations managers now oversee the integration of advanced technologies, including high-efficiency modules, energy storage, and smart grid solutions.

Grid Integration

Grid connectivity and the ability to provide grid support have become integral parts of the role.

Sustainability and Environmental Stewardship

Solar managers are responsible for implementing sustainable practices and minimizing the ecological footprint of solar installations.

Regulatory Compliance

Navigating complex regulatory environments and ensuring compliance with changing policies is a critical aspect.

Data-Driven Decision-Making

Solar operations managers rely on data analytics and real-time monitoring for informed decision-making.

Strategic Planning

The role now encompasses strategic planning to maximize long-term project viability and profitability.

Key Responsibilities

System Performance Optimization

Ensuring optimal energy production and system efficiency through regular maintenance and upgrades.

Environmental Responsibility

Implementing sustainable practices, habitat protection, and environmental impact mitigation.

Technology Integration

Evaluating and integrating emerging technologies for increased efficiency and competitiveness.

Grid Integration

Managing grid connectivity, energy storage, and participation in grid services.

Regulatory Compliance

Staying abreast of changing regulations and ensuring compliance to avoid legal issues.

Financial Management

> Budgeting, cost control, and long-term financial planning to optimize ROI.

> Risk Mitigation

> Identifying and addressing potential risks, including equipment failures and economic fluctuations.

Evolving Skills and Qualities

Technological Proficiency

> Proficiency in solar technologies, energy storage, and data analytics is essential.

Environmental Awareness

> A strong commitment to sustainability and environmental stewardship is increasingly important.

Regulatory Expertise

> Understanding complex regulations and policies is crucial for compliance and strategy.

Data Analysis and Decision-Making

> Data-driven decision-making skills are valuable for optimizing operations.

Adaptability

> Solar operations managers must adapt to changing technologies, market dynamics, and policies.

Leadership and Communication

> Effective leadership and communication skills are essential for managing teams and stakeholders.

Future Trends and Challenges

Decentralization of Energy

> Solar managers may need to adapt to more decentralized energy systems and microgrid management.

Artificial Intelligence (AI) and Automation

AI and automation are likely to play a larger role in predictive maintenance and system optimization.

Climate Resilience

Preparing for and mitigating the effects of extreme weather events will be a growing concern.

Energy Storage Advancements

Ongoing advancements in energy storage technology will impact solar operations.

The role of solar operations managers has evolved significantly, reflecting the changing landscape of the solar energy industry. Modern solar managers must be technologically adept, environmentally conscious, and capable of navigating complex regulatory environments. As the industry continues to evolve, solar operations managers will play a pivotal role in driving the transition to sustainable and efficient solar energy systems.

Looking Toward the Future of Solar Energy

As we conclude this journey into the world of solar energy, it is abundantly clear that solar power is not merely an energy source but a beacon of hope for a sustainable future. Solar energy has evolved from a niche technology into a global powerhouse, reshaping the energy landscape, mitigating climate change, and propelling us toward a more sustainable world.

This comprehensive guide have illuminated the myriad facets of solar energy, from its foundational principles to the complexities of managing large-scale solar operations. We have explored the critical roles of solar operations managers, their evolving responsibilities, and the skills required to thrive in this dynamic field.

The future of solar energy is radiant with promise. As we look ahead, several key trends and imperatives emerge:

Technological Advancements:

Solar technologies will continue to advance, with the development of more efficient modules, innovative energy storage solutions, and sophisticated monitoring systems. Emerging technologies like perovskite solar cells and advanced nanomaterials hold immense potential.

Energy Storage Revolution:

Energy storage will become increasingly integrated into solar installations, allowing for greater energy independence, grid support, and enhanced flexibility. Storage technologies, such as next-gen batteries and thermal storage, will redefine energy management.

Grid Transformation:

Grids will evolve to accommodate the growing share of solar power. Smart grids, microgrids, and grid-forming technologies will enable seamless integration and improved grid resilience.

Environmental Focus:

Environmental sustainability will be a paramount consideration. Solar projects will not only generate clean energy but also embrace sustainable practices, wildlife protection, and habitat restoration.

Policy and Regulation:

Governments worldwide will play a pivotal role in shaping the solar energy landscape. Supportive policies, incentives, and carbon reduction commitments will drive solar adoption and influence project viability.

Decentralization:

Decentralization of energy generation will empower communities and individual consumers to actively participate in energy production. Solar will be a cornerstone of this energy democratization.

Climate Resilience:

Solar operations will need to adapt to changing climate conditions and implement climate-resilient strategies to ensure uninterrupted energy production.

Innovation and Collaboration:

> Collaboration among industries, researchers, and governments will drive innovation and accelerate the transition to renewable energy sources. Cross-sector partnerships will yield breakthroughs in energy technology.

As we stand on the cusp of this solar-powered future, it is imperative that we embrace the boundless potential of solar energy. We must continue to invest in research, innovation, and sustainable practices to harness the sun's energy more efficiently and responsibly.

Solar energy is not just a technology; it is a catalyst for a cleaner, brighter, and more equitable world. It transcends borders, politics, and ideologies, uniting us in a shared vision of a sustainable future. By harnessing the power of the sun, we illuminate a path toward a world where clean energy is abundant, accessible, and essential.

Recap of Key Takeaways

Solar operations managers should incorporate these key takeaways into their strategies to achieve successful and sustainable solar energy projects.

- Efficient solar operations management is vital for maximizing returns and minimizing risks.
- Solar energy is a key player in the transition to sustainable energy sources.
- Solar operations managers play a crucial role in overseeing, optimizing, and maintaining solar energy systems.
- They are responsible for ensuring safety, efficiency, and profitability.
- Effective leadership, communication, and team development are key to building a high-performing team.
- Hiring and training the right personnel with relevant skills and expertise is critical.
- Continual training and development programs keep the team updated on industry advancements.
- Regular team meetings and effective communication enhance collaboration and productivity.

- Managers should foster an open and transparent communication environment.
- Structured team meetings with clear agendas and goals are more efficient and productive.
- Technology tools and platforms facilitate remote collaboration among dispersed teams.
- Setting clear performance expectations and goals is essential.
- Constructive feedback fosters professional growth and improvement.
- Conflict resolution skills are crucial for maintaining team harmony.
- Regular inspections, maintenance, and performance monitoring are key.
- Routine maintenance prevents equipment failures and extends the lifespan of solar assets.
- Predictive maintenance and performance analysis enhance efficiency.
- Effective budgeting ensures financial stability and project viability.
- Budgets should account for operational expenses, maintenance, and contingencies.
- Cost control measures help manage operational expenses.
- Efficient resource allocation optimizes spending and maximizes ROI.
- Long-term financial planning involves forecasting revenue and expenses over the project's lifecycle.
- Planning for contingencies and economic shifts is essential.
- Identify common failure modes and implement robust maintenance plans.
- A maintenance plan includes scheduled inspections, repairs, and spare parts inventory management.
- Predictive and preventive maintenance minimize downtime and costs.
- Develop contingency plans to address unexpected crises and emergencies.
- Effective communication with senior leadership requires clear and concise reporting.
- Present key metrics and performance data to demonstrate project success.
- Accurate reporting and third-party verification enhance project credibility.

- Embrace emerging technologies to enhance efficiency, flexibility, and sustainability.
- Adaptation to changing market dynamics is essential for competitiveness and sustainability.

Be proactive in responding to technological advancements, policy changes, and economic fluctuations.

The journey of solar energy is far from over. It is a journey that beckons us to move forward with determination, creativity, and a deep commitment to preserving our planet for future generations. The future of solar energy is bright, and it is a future worth striving for with unwavering dedication.

Let us embark on this journey together, harnessing the sun's energy to power a sustainable future and illuminate a path toward a world that is cleaner, greener, and more vibrant than ever before.

www.ingramcontent.com/pod-product-compliance
Lightning Source LLC
Chambersburg PA
CBHW072309290526
45794CB00002B/585